Made Healthy in Ministry for Ministry

Made Healthy in Ministry for Ministry

C. JOHN WEBORG

Foreword by
STEPHEN R. GRAHAM AND DAVID W. KERSTEN

PICKWICK *Publications* · Eugene, Oregon

MADE HEALTHY IN MINISTRY FOR MINISTRY

Pickwick Publications
An Imprint of Wipf and Stock Publishers
199 W. 8th Ave., Suite 3
Eugene, OR 97401

www.wipfandstock.com

ISBN 13: 978-1-60899-863-0

Cataloging-in-Publication data:

Weborg, C. John

    Made healthy in ministry for ministry / by C. John Weborg

    p. 134 ; 23 cm. Includes bibliographical references.

    ISBN 13: 978-1-60899-863-0

    1. Clergy—Health and hygiene. 2. Clergy—Mental health. 3. Clergy—Office. 4. Clergy—Appoint, call, and election. 4. Pastoral theology. 5. Evangelical Covenant Church of America—Clergy. I. Title.

BV4398 W4 2011

For Lois

Companion of my life,
now over fifty years

In life, faithful

In hope, enduring

In love, without question

Gift beyond measure

Contents

Foreword

FEW WOULD DENY THE challenges facing pastors today. And few clergy are unaware of the frequency of clergy fatigue, burnout, and discouragement that has afflicted their peers, and perhaps themselves. Pastoral ministry has always been difficult and complex, and it is made more so by the particular financial, cultural, psychological, physical, and spiritual challenges that characterize ministry in the twenty-first century. Because of myriad demands and expectations, pastors often face a crisis of identity. They are expected to be simultaneously CEO of a complex volunteer organization, effective administrator of numerous programs, capable fundraiser, building program overseer, caregiver, and unflappable supervisor of staff.

Those whose work it is to provide care and oversight for pastors recognize the need for training both broad and deep, and the theological schools where that training takes place strain to provide education for all the facets of a pastor's responsibility. The work of being a pastor, as well as training and shepherding pastors, has never been harder. To address these challenges, John Weborg calls pastors (and by implication those who train and shepherd them) back to the center, to the core of pastoral work and identity. Drawing on his lifetime as a pastor, theological educator, counselor, and spiritual director, John shares his unique insights in *Made Healthy in Ministry for Ministry*. The indispensable resources that fortify pastors to carry on their work reside in the pastoral practices of the work itself. In sum, the foundation for ministry *is* the ministry of Word and Sacrament, "the God ordained source and end of the ministry."[1] John argues persuasively that in the *act* of proclamation

1. "Introduction," 2.

ix

and in the *performing* of these rituals is the life-giving source of pastoral ministry itself. In them there is grace for the preacher and celebrant as well as for those who hear and receive. And perhaps there is grace in this necessarily limiting focus. Pastors are called first and foremost to proclaim the Word and celebrate the Sacraments. Doing other things may be necessary, but this ministry of Word and Sacrament is, in an adaptation of the phrase common to the Covenant heritage, "the one thing needful."

As professor of theology and spiritual formation at North Park Theological Seminary (1975–2003), John Weborg's gifts have brought much to the Evangelical Covenant Church. As professor of theology he has educated a whole generation of Covenant pastors in systematic theology; as professor of spiritual formation he has provided his students with tools to build the rich interior lives required to sustain their public ministry; and as chief liturgist for the denomination, he has taught us how to "grant language to the mute,"[2] artfully bringing us before God and naming God's imminent and transcendent presence in our midst. But at the core of his life work, John is a pastor—with his congregation primarily being the community of pastors in the Evangelical Covenant Church. In this volume, John offers a deep and sustaining vision for the art and practice of ministry. The whole church and the pastoral community in particular will be blessed by his wisdom and insight.

Stephen R. Graham
Director, Faculty Development and Initiatives in Theological Education,
Association of Theological Schools
Dean of Faculty at North Park Theological Seminary, 1996–2007

David W. Kersten
Executive Minister, Department of Ordered Ministry, Evangelical
Covenant Church

---

2. "Worshipping Community," (class notes of David W. Kersten, spring quarter, 1982), Professor Weborg quoting Dorothee Soelle.

Preface

IT WAS AN HONOR to be asked to contribute a book to the ongoing ministry to the clergy of the Evangelical Covenant Church, made possible by a grant on Sustaining Pastoral Excellence from the Lilly Endowment. I especially want to extend my deep appreciation to Rev. Daniel R. Pietrzyk, Director, and Dr. Stephen Graham, Dean of Faculty and Professor of American Church History at North Park Theological Seminary, now of the Association of Theological Schools, for inviting me to offer this work and for the encouragement and support necessary for the freedom to complete this project. The Reverend Dr. David Kersten, Executive Minister of the Board of the Ordered Ministry, and the Reverend Carol Lawson, the Director of Staff Ministry—friends of long standing—offered a perspective that only those whose care is from a denominational perspective can offer. Part of the material was presented to a seminar at the Covenant Midwinter Conference in 2007. Former students will recognize themes from class lectures at North Park Theological Seminary, and one Preaching Cohort Retreat segment of Sustaining Pastoral Excellence heard a portion of this book. So did attendees at the North Pacific, Midwest, and Middle East Conference of pastors and spouses. I am most appreciative of the questions and comments from these hearers.

A Luddite such as myself owes much to people skilled in word processing. Two people in particular deserve more than "thank you" for the discipline of deciphering handwriting and for their joyful spirit: Catherine Allicks, my daughter, for beginning the process, and Sharon Weborg, my daughter-in-law, for completing it. Sharon is more than a technician. In bringing this manuscript to publication she showed herself a quality control colleague. Their contribution to this project puts them in my debt, especially their humor and grace, gifts deeply appreciated.

While this work originated in a specific denomination, my intention has been to transcend denominationalism and to present a theological resource for the spiritual lives of those who minister in the diverse Body of Christ. While neither a pastoral theology nor a theology of ordination, this book seeks to surface essential spiritual resources to enable servants of Word and Sacrament to serve the same with faith, hope, and love.

My thanks also to Jamie Rose, whose skill in formatting, patience with detail, and attentiveness to the publisher's discipline sent this manuscript on its way. And to Dr. Paul Koptak who often served as liason.

Finally, to colleagues at Pickwick Publications, my deepest appreciation for receiving and attending to this manuscript with such dispatch and care. Editor Dr. D. Christopher Spinks and I have spoken with some frequency, and for his gracious communication I tender my gratitude. And there are others whose names I know not who have assisted in this process. To you also my thanks.

Fourth Week of Easter, 2011
C. John Weborg

Acknowledgments

G RATEFUL RECOGNITION IS GIVEN to the following authors and/or publishers for permission to quote from their work:

Covenant Publications (Chicago) for use of the quotation from the service of Ordination and Commissioning in *The Covenant Book of Worship*, (2003), pages 402 and 406, and for use of a portion of a baptismal liturgy in *The Covenant Hymnal: A Worshipbook* (1996), page 934.

The *Christian Century* for permission to reprint "All Saints Communion" by Scott Cairns from the *Christian Century* 121.21 (October 19, 2004). Copyright © 2004 *Christian Century*. For more information about the *Century* visit http://christiancentury.org.

Beth Ann Fennelly for use of "My Hundred," first appearing in the *American Poetry Review* 37.5 (September/October 2008).

Kathleen Housley for use of "Lessons for a Young God," a portion of a larger work entitled *Grass*. This excerpt originally appeared in *Image: A Journal of the Arts*, issue 38 (Spring 2003).

Klyne Snodgrass, editor of *Ex Auditu*, and Jon Stock of Wipf and Stock Publishers for their permission to republish my article "Living with God" from *Ex Auditu* 18 (2002) 57–76.

Introduction

Jaroslav Pelikan said that "Tradition is the living faith of the dead; traditionalism is the dead faith of the living. And I suppose I should add, it is traditionalism that gives tradition such a bad name."[1] On first reading, this book might present itself as redundant: traditionalism! But while traditional, the author's intent is to let the tradition be a protection against traditionalism.

Many congregational gathering places nowadays are intentionally lacking in symbols, pulpits, fonts or pools, and communion tables. It is alleged that to secular and sometimes alienated church people such traditional matters communicate nothing or worse, meaningless memories. Instead an open, stage-like theatre, it is argued, is a more familiar setting resembling other venues encountered by secular audiences.[2]

My concern for the tradition, for the rightful place for a pulpit, a communion table, and font or pool is that the acts celebrated at these locations are story-laden. They are the primary shapers of the identity and mission of the assembly, which, in the presence of these three places of ministry, is *not* an audience but a congregation. By virtue of these divinely ordained acts the congregation is *called* by a Word beyond its own local and personal agenda, *named* in the Name of One who calls and then *sends* to continue *his* mission. As with treasured places of memory (our birthplace, place of marriage proposal, etc.) stories and locations go

1. Pelikan, *Vindication of Tradition*, 65.

2. This book is about neither liturgics nor the so-called "worship wars" so this will be elaborated no further. But let me say that the traditional texts—the Creed, the Lord's Prayer, the narrative prayers at baptism and Eucharist—when offered in due reverence, present no intrinsic prohibition to rap, calypso, hip-hop, or jazz than do chant, so long as it is understood that what is done is *service to* Word and Sacrament. The tradition can inhabit diverse forms and thus slips the noose of a stereotypical traditionalism.

together. Remove the locations and the story goes with them. This is not the dead faith of the living but the living faith of the faithful that lives by retelling. As scripture says, "Faith comes by hearing" and is confirmed by what is seen and tasted (Rom 10:17).

By locating ministry in Word and Sacrament it is most appropriate to speak of those who minister them as servants of the Word and Sacrament. They are not sellers or marketers of the Word and Means of Grace as though they were products dependant primarily on the savvy of a salesperson or the skills of a stage personality. Servants of the Word and Sacrament are dependant on the God who ordained such Word and Sacrament in the first place and on whose promise alone the validity of any ordered ministry rests.

This in no way removes the personality or presence of the servant of Word and Sacrament. It is only to locate the source of his or her vocation and to be able to rest, literally to rest, in the Word and Sacrament made efficacious in the promise of the Triune God. That gift is not traditionalism, but as my offering intends to show, in the tradition at its fruit bearing best, both for pastors and congregations, as they are served by and serve the Word and Sacrament as the history and hope of anything called ministry.

Therefore my purpose is to show that the things we are ordained to do—preach the Word and administer the Sacraments—are the very things ordained by the Holy Trinity to sustain both the minister and ministry. The vocational ministry of the church may be unique in this, namely that the very work of the ministry—Word and Sacrament—is the God ordained source and end of the ministry. To hear most people speak it, they seek sustenance for doing their work elsewhere than in their work; release from their work is needed to find sustenance for their work. Their work is a drain, often a source of hatred to the point of living by the exclamation made popular some years ago: "take this job and shove it."

Don't mistake my thesis. I am not idealizing church ministry. Nor am I seeking to remove it from the tensions and stresses of the workday world. Ministry is subject to all of the hazards the "helping professions" are likely to encounter. And I am not arguing that church ministry is so continually rewarding and enriching that one needs to observe no Sabbath, take no day off or enjoy the annual vacation. Anyone who ignores this temporal and physical observance is in plain violation of scripture let alone God's own intentional Sabbath.

My point is to inquire just how the things we are ordained to do—Word and Sacrament—are the very things that give intent and extent to the ministry. Lest readers may think my purview is reduced to ritual performance and the creation of a priestly elite, I want to show how the *intent* of Word and Sacrament makes a ministry possible in the first place for both pastors and congregations. As for *extent*, it just may be found liberating to know that the basics of ministry—Word and Sacrament—speak of the special competence of pastors in particular and congregations in general. Word and Sacrament mark a boundary to what we in the ministry are called to do and it is for our spiritual, physical and mental health that we enjoy the grace of this limitation. I hope when I am finished that I have communicated just what a magnificent intent and extent God has given us who minister at the pulpit, font or pool and table.

My basic argument or purpose will be intensified by showing how these three locations of ministry show forth the intent and extent of ministry. All three locations—pulpit, font or pool and table—are ministries of the word made speech and the word made visible. All three locations have a "no more, no less" about the speaking done at each. The speaker of the word in sermon knows that the words he or she speaks holds the Word that made all things in the beginning and eventually became flesh. The speaker is more owned by the Word than owns the Word. We speak in borrowed tongue. As for the font or pool and table, we only repeat the words of the One who commanded us to do these things. The acts of water, bread and wine cannot be ad-libbed. The words are not ours. That is in part what I mean by extent: our speech is limited by and to Jesus' words. The intent is to speak them, to continue his speaking. The extent is his words. We have nothing else to say.

There is more to ministry than what I have introduced. There is administration, bearing rule in the church, visitation, counseling and more. But in one way or another they are an outgrowth of and lead back to Word and Sacrament. Those two things are the basics. If we stick to them, I will argue, we have hope, even in the ministry for life and salvation. Just how other acts of ministry relate to Word and Sacrament will receive attention in due course.

My intended outcome is the spiritual maturation of the practitioner in the practice of ministry, contending that such maturity requires that one be a hearer of the Word before one is a preacher/teacher of the Word; that one fully appreciates one's baptismal identity as a baptizer of others; and that one embraces to the fullest extent possible that one is a communicant before and while one is a celebrant of the Eucharist. I am interested as to how these three locations of ministry and three acts of ministry serve as the transcendental grounds for the competence, character, and integrity of those in vocational ministry.[3]

But let us admit to a complexity not at all hospitable to a more pragmatic American culture oriented toward a more quantitative and less narrative form of leadership performance and organizational self-understanding. E. Brooks Holifield's *God's Ambassadors: A History for the Christian Clergy in America* is both comprehensive in scope and precise in its script. Attending equally to Protestant and Roman Catholic clergy, he maintains from page 4 to page 348 that the one constant has been that congregational leadership has been the consistent work of pastors. There the consistency ends.

What has in great part provoked the inconsistency according to Holifield is the way pastors view their calling (a profession, a vocation, a priest, a prophet, a CEO, an evangelist, a pastoral therapist, or any combination thereof) is the tension between immanence and transcendence.[4] As Holifield further elaborates "this theological paradox of the immanent-transcendent God" makes any form of evaluation difficult since pastors are to be in the world but not of it. Such a paradox did not fare well in the face of business criteria and salesmen models in contrast to someone who perceived his/her role in terms of the stewardship of a transcendent story and a prophetic critique of life in the world. In fact

---

3. Two books by William Willimon explore these themes: *Calling and Character* and *Pastor: Theology and Practice of Ordained Ministry*. I owe these words to Bishop Willimon.

4. Holifield, *God's Ambassadors*, 4. I want also to commend G. Lee Ramsey Jr., *Preachers and Misfits*. Ramsey's study shows the outworking of one dominant model of the pastor: preacher. Beyond that, it is an education in the vast literature of a geographical region and a challenging encounter with the pastoral vocation told by writers of literary skill and insight embedded in a distinct cultural ethos (the South). The complexity of pastoral and ecclesiastical identity is revealed in multiple sociological settings.

the tension between immanence and transcendence has led clergy in nearly every generation to view their calling as one in crisis.[5]

The cogency of Holifield's argument, that a mystery inheres in the ministry that defies definition, measurement and planning because it embodies the nexus of the transcendent in the immanent, confronted me in a specific way in Princeton, Illinois, in the 1970s. Serving the Evangelical Covenant Church, I was about to make a pastoral visit to a patient in Perry Memorial Hospital. Stepping out of the elevator a nurse recognized me, stopped me, and asked me to visit another patient who had just been informed that she had a terminal illness. I had never met the patient. I have no memory what I said. But the incident coalesced the issues that Holifield, in part at least, has identified.

For one thing, the ministry plays an alien language game, to borrow some words prevalent in the thought of Wittgenstein. The doctor had spoken of going from life to death; I had come to speak of going from death to life. This is gospel sense, not common sense.

A second reflection that gradually emerged was that the instruments of ministry were Word, Water, Bread, and Wine.[6] That's all. But that's more than enough considering the divine institution of each means of communication and the divine promises attached to each means of communication. My hands held these divinely instituted means and my mouth could speak the promises. But neither my mouth nor my hands controlled the outcome. The Triune God does.

In the meantime those of us who serve Word and Sacrament are served by these same gifts whose sufficiency we come to know as we serve in the faith that acts in love, the transcendent pleased to inhabit the immanent. The ministry is never in the possession of the ministry. To get possessive is to begin the downward spiral to ill health.

Appropriately, Jackson Carroll's *God's Potters: Pastoral Leadership and the Shaping of Congregations* is a most congenial sociological partner to Holifield's work and should be read in tandem with it. Attentive to the themes of profession versus vocation and the distinctions among the callings—i.e., personal calling to be a Christian, a secret calling to take up the ministry, providential call, viz., the equipping of a person with gifts and an ecclesiastical call, the official call by a church to ministry—Carroll gives sustained theological and sociological treatment to

5. Holifield, *God's Ambassadors*, 9.

6. When pastorally appropriate, the service of healing and anointing may be offered.

these issues.[7] Holifield writes historically about the consistency of pastoral leadership of congregations, Carroll of developing congregational cultures as a locus of God's revelation. The potter theme in 2 Corinthians 4:7 suggests that congregations be thought of as clay jars and pastors as God's potters.[8] The astounding thing is that the earthen vessels reveal the transcendent, the twin themes generative of the tension that Holifield finds at work in any effort to pin down the nature and function of the ministerial office. Or is it just a function?

Carroll shows how the twin themes of transcendence and immanence equally bedevil congregational self-understanding, especially in American culture. The voluntary principle dominates American religious life surrounded as it is by consumer notions of choice and preference. Loyalty cannot be assumed. So, *theologically*, a congregation is the Body of Christ charged with continuing his work in the world, inviting people to receive the offer of salvation and to become fellow workers in the mission. *Sociologically*, congregations are voluntary associations that are important producers of social capital; networks where friendships can be developed and perspectives can be shaped by worship and study. Thus a culture can be produced by a congregation.[9] This is Carroll's way of specifying the transcendent (the theological) and the immanent (the sociological) dimensions of a congregation. But does the congregation have a theological identity, rooted in the sacramental narrative of naming, calling, and sending in baptism and reconfirmed in the narrative of the Eucharist?

Perhaps a theological question: Are there volunteers for Jesus in the New Testament? It's the word "voluntary" that needs careful nuancing in the American setting since it is a complete violation of a baptismal theology in which one is engrafted into Christ, into Christ's mission and ultimately into the *missio Dei*. Furthermore, without a missional and congregational theology rooted in baptism, the congregation is in danger of becoming hardly anything other than a service club, in which case the transcendent dimension is lacking. The New Testament's stress is on calling, sending, and continuing a mission, *not* one's own but that of God made plain in Jesus and called forth by the Holy Spirit. The Spirit equips the baptized with the requisite gifts for ministry and pastors who

7. Carroll, *God's Potters*, 22.

8. Ibid., 2.

9. Ibid., 97.

enable the baptized to find and do their ministry. The entire Christian enterprise challenges any categorization and ultimately any form of comprehensive management. It is the embodied tension of transcendence in immanence, the hidden-revealed mystery of Ephesians 3.

I'll let Barbara Brown Taylor proclaim this mystery vocationally with Word, Water, Bread, and Wine:

> Because I am a preacher, it is through a preacher's eyes that I tend to see that work, but because I am a baptized Christian too, it is from that perspective that I write. Either way, my job remains that same; to proclaim the good-news of God in Christ and to celebrate the sacrament of God's presence in the world. Those two jobs are described as clearly in the baptismal vows as they are in the ordination vows, which gives Christians a common vocation. Our job is to stand with one foot on earth and one in heaven, with the double vision that is the gift of faith, and to say out of our own experience that reality is not flat but deep, not opaque but transparent, not meaningless but shot full of grace for those with the least willingness to believe it.[10]

My plan proceeds in two parts. Chapter 1 is my basic spiritual theology. Its focus is living *with*, not just for God. Biblical characters found this to be a contentious, compelling, combative, and conducive vocation implicit in the fulfillment of their calling. No less so for us. Thus this essay, once before published concerning formation in the course of theological education, provides background and foreground for the remainder of the book, especially the notion of narrative coherence. The book is not an exposition of chapter 1, but chapter 1 animates the soul of him or her who serves out their ecclesiastical calling and so animates this book as well.

Chapters 2–7 pick up vocational vulnerabilities, all having to do with hands. Hands are laid on in ordination. Such recipients are authorized to handle the Word, Water, Bread, and Wine and persons put themselves in trust into our hands. Each "handling" receives a chapter, not as description of task but as to how the task embodies the law and gospel of the God whose narrative such authorized persons continue to serve and by which they are served. Said differently, such authorized persons allow themselves to be disciplined by a story to a story, the story

---

10. Taylor, *Preaching Life*, 12.

of the one and same God whose authorizing name is Father, Son, and Holy Spirit.

I must add a clarifying note as to the crucial role of narrative in identity formation, which accounts for numerous such references in this book. In James R. Nieman's essay "The Theological Work of Denominations," the question is posed as to why identity formation, theological or otherwise, should have a narrative quality. This lengthy citation is justified:

> . . . narratives are cultural constructions with the distinct ability to shape language toward a compact, shared, but paradoxical story reality. On the one hand, narratives create a sense of home, using words that build a world of the familiar and predictable, with all the richness and alternatives we might expect there. On the other hand, to create a sense of possibility, using words that allow us not only to anticipate problems (subjunctive potential) but also to imagine new ones (subversive potential). (a) Put another way, good narratives have both a mythic and a parabolic character. While the mythic side of narratives mediates and reconciles, resolving tensions and evoking stability, the (b) parabolic side challenges and disrupts, shattering any complacency with unforeseen and even disturbing possibilities. Narrative requires these two aspects since both are intertwined in all life.[11]

In life as in ministry, the mythic (the basic structure of the story from creation through redemption to eschatology, especially when the "story follows the script" and expectations are served) is told and retold and the parabolic (the challenges and questions; the story, exile and exodus; lament and praise; anger psalms and trust; the night of betrayal and the morning of resurrection) are intertwined. Preaching includes both. Liturgy enacts both. Prayer prays both the mythic and parabolic in the same prayer, e.g., Psalm 22. Living for God entails living with the same God, both of which inhabit a narrative coherence that plays itself out in scripture and into whose hands the lives and times of congregations and persons have been entrusted.

---

11. Nieman, *Church, Identity, and Change*, 644. Reference (a) is to Bruner, *Making*, 3–13; reference (b) is to Crossan, *Dark Interval*, 51–57. I must commend this rich book of denominational case studies with theological and sociological commentary, especially as regards identity formation.

~∞~

Meditations or the nucleus of meditations are distributed through-out the book, some in the body of the text, some at the end. Here is the first.

> We declare to you what was from the beginning, what we have heard, what we have seen with our own eyes, what we looked at and touched with our hands, concerning the word of life—this life was revealed, and we have seen and testify to it, and declare to you the eternal life that was with the Father and was revealed to us—we declare to you what we have seen and heard so that you also may have fellowship with us; and truly our fellowship is with the Father and with his Son Jesus Christ. 1 John 1:1–2

BODY HANDLERS

We are body handlers—not in the crude sense of ambulance chasers, traffickers in human slave trade, or smuggling third world persons in death-trap vans or cargo holds.

We are body handlers.

Personally

By greeting others, the embrace of spouses, care of in-fants, or, on the depraved side, by abuse or threat.

Vocationally

We bathe, give back rubs, draw blood, administer injections.

We baptize, anoint with oil, commend the dead with the laying on of hands, and handle the body of Christ in the Eucharist. We lift hands in blessing over a people.

How do body handlers experience body handling?

Is a surgeon about to make a first incision or try a new procedure as terrified as when Luther offered his first mass?

What rushes up in the mind of a first year medical stu-dent about to meet his or her first cadaver? The first time a pastor holds the bread and wine to be consecrated? The first time a parent holds a newborn?

The body—inviting and intimidating; fascinating and frightening.

God is a body handler.

In the creation by Michelangelo the finger of God and the finger of Adam do not touch.

In Jesus God touched the human body, first in Jesus the Word made flesh, and through Jesus all sorts and conditions of bodies.

In Christ all creation was touched and taken up in the mystery of God's full blessing on the world he had made. Nothing was to be untouched by God.

In Jesus' baptism all waters were sanctified and in his burial all graves were taken up into the Word made flesh.

Body handling carries a fear of contagion with it. But body handling can have the opposite effect: what is touched can be consecrated to the full gift of life God intended.

Let us say then that body handling is a priestly act as well as a vocational and professional art or parental, spousal, or friendly act.

While body handling can become burdensome, cross-bearing when the embodied person is truly embraced, it is a gift of grace to know that our calling is to *care* in every way but not to *cure* every person's embodied needs.

1

Living with God

Thesis

THE OBVIOUS VOCATION OF a theological seminary is the preparation of persons *to do ministry*: preach, teach, administer the sacraments and other rites, train the laity, and serve the larger church. The more subtle, maybe even more foundational vocation of the seminary, is to prepare the *persons* who do ministry to grow in the grace and knowledge of our Lord Jesus Christ (2 Pet 3:18), capacitate them continually to make a fearless personal moral inventory, and to practice those habits of life conducive to personal and public virtue.

My thesis is that we prepare for life in the course of life. The period of seminary education does not put the life of the seminarian on hold, restraining whatever it is, either of ease or adversity, that might intrude itself into the theologian's life. Experience provides the lived material to work with, provided one is willing to experience the experience that memory makes available.[1] Kierkegaard called this the task of becoming a "subjective thinker,"[2] which requires "the grave strenuosity of faith."[3] The threat and promise of this entire enterprise is to have the stamina, steadfastness, and will to experience experience.

1. Weborg, "Spiritual Formation," 3.
2. Kierkegaard, *Concluding Unscientific Postscript*, 73, 84, 267–70.
3. Ibid, 188.

Abstract

Living *for* God is the more conventional way of describing the Christian life. Such discipleship calls for discernment, sacrifice, zeal, commitment, conviction and a devotional life supportive of these demands. Living *with* God is a concomitant factor of discipleship. Persistence, perseverance, protest, gratitude, a capacity for disillusionment as well a devotion, and at times a dogged game of hide and seek all make living with God a venture of faith continuing to act in love. As the Christian serves in faith acting in love, he/she waits in hope for God to vindicate God's promise of presence, fruit, and covenant loyalty. The structure of the theology presented here, both as *prima* and *secunda* is theocentric rather than Christocentric. In the process of living with God while at the same time living for God, faith, hope, and love are kept alive as the Holy Spirit, by means of Word and Sacrament, attests that "the renewal of creation has been wrought by the self-same Word who made it in the beginning."[4]

THE PROBLEM

Delineating the Issue

Barry and Connolly say, "Resistance is a critical element in the development of every interpersonal relationship."[5] Resistance inhabits the space between the perceived need for change and the risk required to address it. Persons know the need long before it is brought into speech, adding to the accumulating tension contributing to its repression. No less than in significant human relations, the same agony often accompanies the negotiation of a relationship with God.

According to Barry and Connolly the accumulated literature of spiritual direction specifies five crucial areas where resistance can assert itself in uninvited ways. Variations on these five themes are ubiquitous:

1. Issues relating to the image of God with which each directee has lived. This can be related to experiences of power, gender, maturation levels, laxity, scrupulosity, etc.

2. Fear of losing one's relationship with God, including being overcome by the immensity of God, especially if one cannot pray in

---

4. Athanasius, *On the Incarnation*, 1:1.

5. Berry and Connolly, *Practice*, 81.

mature ways, expressing genuine feelings, memories, grievances, etc. Directees can be taught that there is no "right" way to pray, a kind of hidden code that needs to be found in order to legitimate one's prayers. I find the staple antidote to this fear is to "read, mark, learn, and inwardly digest" the prayers in Scripture.[6]

3. In the maturation of relationships, differences between oneself and the other, including God, may intensify. Expectations get undermined or even derailed in the process of allowing the other to be other than one's image of them. In turn the painful process of letting one's self be other than one's projection of one's ideal self is set in motion. Here the capacity for receptivity to grace as the ground of freedom towards God, self, and others is the crucial factor. The God who is other than one's image of God can be lived with in the process of mature differentiation, and the self who is other than one's ideal self can be lived with by grace.

4. There is realistic fear of texts calling for a demanding discipleship. Some examples might be: "be angry and sin not," "sell what you have, give to the poor and follow me," "in everything give thanks," or "pray without ceasing."

5. The presence of secret sins.[7]

It is striking that three of these five categories relate directly to the God issue. If the issues in the first three categories are not dealt with appropriately, the last two will fall victim to the first three. For example, if one's images of God are drawn from the field of jurisprudence or from authoritarian models only, one might not have the confidence required to pursue the risky demands of some of the discipleship texts. The risk of displeasing God is too great and the risk of failure in one's own eyes is too immediate. The decisive issues in formation and direction are theocentric in origin and outcome.

With the permission of a former student of mine, I am presenting a "case" this early in the paper to demonstrate the inherent theocentric issues in trying to come to terms with the demands of the Christian life.[8] The "case" should make it painfully apparent how early in life these

---

6. *Book of Common Prayer*, proper 28.

7. Berry and Connolly, *Practice*, 82–91.

8. See "Bringing Spiritual."

formational issues are engaged. This "case" concerns missionary kids (MKs) and their need for coping capacities dealing with long separations from families, both immediate and extended. The event in question is leaving home (the place of parental missionary service) to attend a boarding school where other MKs are educated. The single event of leaving home involves four losses: relationships (parents and friends), material (familiar objects and surroundings), control (familiar routines, systems of interaction), and role (a sense of one's place in a social network).

The student enlists the help of Ruth E. Van Reken, who underwent the same process as she tried to verbalize the process.

1. Protest: Parents say the plane ride would be fun; (it was tears all the way).

2. Despair: I quit crying at bedtime; it doesn't do any good. The teachers think I'm well adjusted. They don't know that I've given up.

3. Detachment: Withdrawal of investment in parental relationships. It's as if I have to count you as dead.

As can be imagined, the thought of reunion with parents is not very comforting.

Spiritual formation issues enter the picture when missionary circles stress, "victory only" spirituality, masking grief and anger.[9] Painful feelings are a sign of spiritual weakness and worst of all, people are to spiritualize their experiences rather than to express true feelings. It is not hard to conceptualize the toll this takes or the future occasions when this will erupt in anger and opposition to the church and the faith that landed the family in a place where the faith failed them (as the perception goes).

Van Reken, according to the student, argues that these losses are tied directly to God since God is the one who calls to missionary service and is the one whom they serve. Pain issues and faith issues coalesce. "To question the pain is to question God."[10] Expression of pain by MKs was rebellion against God. "Pain and faith was antithetical," one MK said, "If someone had been . . . able to accept my questions about why I felt so rotten if God wanted my parents to do what they did, instead of speaking platitudes about God taking care of everything if you trust

9. Van Reken, *Letters*, 5, 9, 37; cited in "Bringing Spiritual," 5–6.
10. Manning, *Don't Take My Grief*, 78; quoted in "Bringing Spiritual," 8.

him, I might have found an easier way through those years. Instead, I ended up feeling . . . [that] my pain was a consequence of my failure to trust God. But I didn't know how to trust anymore than I was and the pain didn't go away. [The] lesson I learned was that you couldn't count on God . . . That is a very lonely place to be—not able to trust people or to trust God."[11]

Nearly every one of Barry's and Connolly's five areas of resistance are included in some way in this "case." The theocentric issues dominate. Living with God, especially if it is one's parents' God, is more than can be expected. What is more, missionaries undergo some kind of formation during their preparation. Apparently it escaped everyone's notice that the image of God, let alone concept of God, communicated by home, church, and school of preparation was unbiblical and for that reason could not serve as a conversation partner. As this case shows, the consequences were for a lifetime.

Intellectual and spiritual dishonesty can be mitigated in part by a theological education that stresses God as both subject and as subject matter, as someone lived with and as well as lived for. A relationship as symbiotic as the ancient formulation, the law of prayer is the law of believing (*lex orandi, lex credendi*) is required. This in turn requires a theological approach that can hold *theologia prima* and *theologia secunda* in tandem as the seminary prepares persons for ecclesiastical service. Such persons can develop a capacity for an intellectual integrity and a spiritual integrity that can permit God as both subject and subject matter mutually to inform and interrogate each other in the life of the person living with God, a life that does not go on hold even in seminary.

For now, a brief distinction needs to be drawn between *theologia prima* and *theologia secunda*.

PERSPECTIVE

Distinction

Theologia prima as primary theology is speech to God. It is speech in the second person, direct and personal—like face to face. When God is the conversation partner it is not a conversation between equals. Primordial thinking is its modus operandi.

11. Van Reken, "Possible," 7; quoted in "Bringing Spiritual," 9.

Philosophically, with John Macquarrie, one may specify three types of thinking: 1) *Calculative thinking* clearly differentiates the subject from the object. Control belongs to the subject, objectivity inhabits the distance between subject and object, and instrumentality—the subject's use of the object—is the *telos*. 2) *Existential thinking* does not aim at use or distance. It is subject-to-subject conversation wherein each shares in the same human being and there is reciprocal participation in the revelation each one unfolds. 3) *Primordial thinking* is also subject-to-subject but in a unique fashion: one of the parties is transcended, mastered, overcome, but in such a way so as to be neither objectified nor necessarily robbed of personhood. In fact, the overwhelming of one being by another may be a time of great freedom, as in the case of grace, or great *angst*, as in the case of guilt.[12]

Primordial engagements are freighted with ambiguity: attraction and alienation, desire and dread, intimacy and intimidation. In an exquisite *andacht* ("devotion") on the encounter between St. John of the Apocalypse and the glorified Jesus Christ, the one before whom St. John fell down as though dead, Johann Albrecht Bengel comments on Jesus' gesture of laying his hand on St. John and telling him, "Fear not, I am the first and the last, the living one; I died, and behold I am alive for evermore, and I have the keys of Death and Hades" (Rev 1:17b–18), that St. John was both frightened and fortified.[13] The ambiguity of this experience and the ambivalence felt by St. John bear striking resemblance to the encounters of Hannah (1 Sam 1–2), Isaiah (ch. 6), St. Peter, unworthy of the miraculous catch of fish (Luke 5), and St. Paul at his conversion (Acts 9). So astounded is St. Paul by this sovereign act of grace and vocation that he appropriates an unlikely metaphor: ἐκτρώματι—a miscarriage or an abortion of an apostle (cf. 1 Cor 15:8). More conventionally translated, St. Paul is one who is untimely born, who is the least of the apostles and unfit to be called such (1 Cor 15:8–9). St. Paul is living with a grace that defies his categories yet daring him to believe it. Too good to be true! Grace easily becomes its own worst enemy and becomes the grounds for its own defeat, basically because it is unbelievable! It frightens yet fortifies—fearful of being presumptive at such grace

---

12. Macquarrie, *Principles*, 91–95. Marquarrie cites his dependence on Martin Heidegger's *Was Ist Metaphysik?*

13. Bengel, *Sechzig Erbaulicher Reden*, 48, 63.

yet fortified by its gratuitousness. Live with it by living by it. Grace defies any calculus.

Theologia secunda is speech about God. It is speech in the third person. It has some commonality with calculative thinking in that it works, not so much with a subject but with subject matter. Secondary theology seeks an appropriate method and a coherent "system" of the Christian faith such as one might find in Tillich's *Systematic Theology*. If I were to give a schematic comparison between the two approaches, but not in any way exhaustive, it would look something like this:[14]

Theologia Prima	*Theologia Secunda*
silence	conceptual clarity
experience seeking understanding	epistemology: faith seeking understanding
Bible stories, screams, parables	hermeneutics, exegesis
injustice, anger seeking vindication	theodicy
guilt seeking remission	atonement
death, grief seeking reprieve	resurrection
persons in search of community	initiation and ecclesiology
good fortune seeking praise	Eucharist
hope deferred	eschatology
prayer, protest, stymied thoughts	propositions, resolution
yet stubborn resolve	

Theologia prima resists systematization and forestalls premature conclusions. When *theologia secunda* is trumpeting the consistency of its logic and hermeneutics, *theologia prima* will provide the text that will not fit! Helmut Thielicke says that "theology betrays its deepest secrets in moments of inconsistency."[15] *Theologia prima* knows that and finds it to be a source of suffering, an occasion to tempt intellectual integrity searching for the quick fix, secretly wishing perhaps that Sebastian

---

14. Leclercq, *Love of learning*, develops a contrast between monastic theology and scholastic theology. Previously I have published a similar attempt to work at this way of making distinctions in Colyer, *Evangelical Theology*, 158–60.

15. Thielicke, *Modern Faith*, 99.

Moore was wrong when he said to Kathleen Norris that God behaves differently in the Psalms than in systematic theology![16]

Theologia prima and *theologia secunda* are not alternatives. They belong together as do *lex orandi, lex credendi*. Education is painful, learning requires unlearning, concepts need to be distinguished from convictions, and the theology has to be freed from the need to personalize everything: every question addressed to the theology is not an attack on the thinker's person. Differentiation of self from one's thought without succumbing either to indifference or to total separation from one's intellectual activity is a painful process and belongs in a theological education.

Noel Annan, writing about the emergence of dons at Oxford and Cambridge, says that the one task of the university is to cultivate a capacity for learning.[17] Granted, the radical exclusivity of the proposition may not be entirely satisfying because skills, practice, and knowledge are also the anticipated fruits of an education. Yet the educated person is one who cultivates a capacity for learning, including the painful aspects of recognizing one's blinders, ignorance, and at times unwillingness to recognize, identify, and confront one's resistance to learning.

If education means cultivating the capacity for learning, spiritual formation concerns itself with the capacity for receptivity to the work of the Triune God. In the tradition of Pietism (North Park's native air) there was talk of the conviction of sin as the Holy Spirit confronted believers with the law and gospel. It is natural to resist such exposure because one has no preunderstanding of how deep or to what extent one's life will be laid bare (Heb 4:12–13). The most painful part is to admit the truthfulness of the conviction (Ps 51:4). To do so is to repent and repentance is the formational equivalent of admitting the need to unlearn something or to admit that what one had treated as fact is only prejudice, and in social ethics, mores, not moral stipulation.

At that point the construction job that is one's life can implode. Implosion is one of the ways God uses to free persons by the truth for the truth. In some ways education and formation are one long (lifelong, hopefully) process of crisis stewardship: education and formation are never freed from their nemesis, namely a seemingly intractable capacity for resistance to both grace and knowledge. The crisis of which one is a steward is epistemological: the process of knowing is a process of

16. Norris, "Paradox," 222.

17. Annan, *Dons*, 3.

revelation, of uncovering hidden truth whether hidden by ignorance, prejudice, or the plain cussed resistance of "I have my mind made up; don't confuse me with the facts." St. Paul warns against a darkened understanding due to ignorance and hardness of heart. Classical theology called this the noetic effects of sin. Put plainly, sinners are characterized as unteachable (Eph 4:18). The consequence of such hardness and darkened understanding is the loss of sensitivity and abandonment to a behavior that dehumanizes oneself and victimizes others (Eph 4:19). No wonder persons want deliverance from a theological education and a sustained exposure to formation. It is a continual exposure to one's ignorance and, worse, the preferential option for ignorance. Ignorance seems easier.

The mystery of having the capacity for education and formation, for grace and knowledge, is at the heart of the matter. The development of such a capacity requires that *theologia prima* and *theologia secunda* be allowed their rightful place in the economy of a theological education so that theologs may know in a healthy fashion that God is both subject and subject matter. Theologs also need to know that to subsume subject into subject matter is to eliminate any possibility of a relationship with God. Subject matter thrives in the atmosphere of calculative thinking and third person speech. Theology or subject matter is unresponsive to human need and unable finally to answer all of the questions posed to it. Yet the pursuit of the final answer, like Stephen Hawking's search for the theory of everything, has a flaw: who can certify the omniscience to claim such a feat? My view is that when calculative thinking reaches its end result, it too finds that not everything is calculable. For theologians there is always a text that does not fit or an experience that is minimized so that one can supply a packaged answer, as Job's friends. I think Gödel's proof in mathematical theory is instructive for theologians: "This proof states that within any rigidly logical mathematical system, there are certain questions that cannot be proved or disproved on the basis of axioms within the system. Therefore it is uncertain that the basic axioms of arithmetic will not give rise to contradictions."[18]

Is it not also possible that basic axioms in theology, if always taken to their logical conclusion, can give rise to contradictions? That certain issues in theology cannot be proved or disproved on the basis of axioms within the system? When primordial thinking rather than calculative

---

18. Barnes-Svarney, *New York*, 42.

thinking faces some of these questions, primordial thinking seeks theological perspective more than a theological position. The reason is a that theolog has to live with God as well as learn about God.

I have no idea why God closed Hannah's womb (1 Sam 1:6–7), yet that assertion becomes a pretext for Peninnah to turn it into a *cause celebre* (1 Sam 1:6–7) and to continue such harassment year after year. Is the closing of Hannah's womb a verdict rendered by divine revelation? If so is God aware that it was a setup for Hannah's daily horror? Is it a human interpretation of a physical condition attributed to divine activity? Does such an attribution mask a notion of punishment for sin latent in it? Can a modern woman, afflicted with infertility, read this text without some kind of horror and without becoming jealous of Hannah who finally did conceive? Does such a woman get caught in a vortex of centripetal and centrifugal forces wanting to worship a God whom she distrusts?

Theologia secunda argues that God is sovereign, free, and in some theological systems, accountable to no one. *Theologia prima* asks God for some accounting, not only for the sake of humans but for God's sake.

PRACTICE

The next section, albeit in sketchy fashion, develops how the perspective sketched above might provide a method (*theologia prima*) to deal with the central issue in forming and living the Christian life (theocentricity) and how this contour of spiritual formation might become part of formation teaching and practice in theological education.

I. The two testaments of the Christian bible show a narrative coherence. In both testaments there is clear evidence that poets, prophets, historians, gospel and epistle writers were disciplined by a story to a story even as the story was appropriated "to tradition" new traditions. This may be *illustrated* in the following texts:

Intratestamentally

Jeremiah (7:21–26, 11:3–5 and 16:14–15) uses the Exodus narrative as a basis for showing how a redeemed people forgot their redeemer and lost track of their vocation to be redeeming. When Jeremiah engages their ingratitude (2:13) he does so using Deuteronomy 6:10–15 to show

how Israel has taken over cisterns they did not dig as though they were children intoxicated with entitlement.

Deuteronomy 4:9–24 and 8:2–18, preoccupied as they are with the perils of forgetfulness, makes clear to Israel that their forgetfulness of God's election and exodus jeopardizes their existence. Forgetfulness of God was a repeated concern of the psalmists (Pss 55:11, 59:11, 78:7 and 103:2).

Hosea 12:2–4 retrieves the Jacob story as a heuristic device to bring continuing internecine injustice and conflict in the nation to public exposure.

Intertestamentally

The two genealogies of Jesus are a story of many stories providing the Christian reader with a narrative coherence of the two testaments and forecloses on any identity description of Jesus that ignores the Old Testament.

When Mathew composes the narrative of the slaughter of the children by Herod (2:16ff) he does so by appropriating the Rachel story (Gen 35:16–21; death during Benjamin's birth) and Jeremiah's use of it (Jer 31:15; Rachel watching the trek into exile). For Matthew, Rachel continues to weep during Herod's time and the later time of Matthew's congregation.

The text on ecclesiology in 1 Peter 2:9–10 is constructed out of Exodus 19:6 (priestly kingdom and holy nation) and Hosea 1:9–10 (once you were no people and now you are God's people) among others.

The good shepherd and hireling themes of John 10 are in contrast to Jeremiah 23:1–5 and Ezekiel 34.

II. One way to account for the narrative coherence of the two testaments of Christian scripture is that the one and the same God is active in both. The one and same God who called and sent Israel into its ministry called and sent Jesus of Nazareth. The one and the same God who brought Israel out of Egypt brought Jesus out of the tomb.[19]

Passages where God is the subject (illustrative only):

In relation to sending the Son: John 5:24, 30; 6:44; 17:3, 18, 21, 23; 1 John 4:4

---

19. Jensen, *Systematic Theology*, 42–46; Janowski, "One God"; and Holmgren, *Old Testament*.

In relation to the atonement: 2 Cor 5:7; Rom 3:25, 8:3; John 3:16

In relation to the resurrection (God raised Jesus): Acts: 2:23–24, 36; 3:15; 5:30–31; Rom 1:1–5; 8:11; Gal 1:1; Phlm 2:5–11; 1 Cor 6:41

Salvation history: Hebrews 1:1–2 ("God who . . .")

In relation to the Holy Spirit: John 10:26; Gal 4:4

III. When Jesus prayed, he prayed to the one and same God to whom Abraham, Hagar, Moses, Hannah, Judas Maccabeus and others had prayed. In this he was instructed and inspired by the story to which and by which he had been disciplined.

The theocentric character of Jesus' life comes to full expression in Hebrews 5:7–10: "In the days of his flesh, Jesus offered up prayers and supplications, with loud cries and tears, to the one who was able to save him from death, and he was heard because of his reverent submission. Although he was a Son, he learned obedience through what he suffered, and having been made perfect, he became the source of eternal salvation for all who obey him, having been designated by God a high priest according to the order of Melchizedek."

The one to whom he prayed was the one whose work he had come to do and whose words he was to speak. This one to whom he prayed was the one to whom Moses and Hannah had prayed. Like them he appropriated words from the tradition to "tradition" his own life with God. Note the Psalms that are quoted from the cross.

Jesus could engage this One in ways as vigorous as his predecessors. For example, Psalm 22 begins by asking why God had forsaken his servant. In verse 3 it proclaims the holiness of God. In one prayer there is accusation and acclamation. The accusation in the English text is prefaced by "yet" followed in verse 6 with a "but," in verse 9 with a "yet," all showing a prayer processing what it meant to live with God. Confusion shares space with confidence. The theology Jesus inherited permitted the process of thinking out loud, praying oneself from confusion to confidence if not always to certainty and clarity. Was it because of this history of truthful prayer, of story-laden phrases and references, that Jesus could say, "Father, into your hands I commit my Spirit"? The location of that text in Psalm 31 is preceded by a lament at being the scorn of enemies, an object of horror, and the victim of a treacherous scheme. It is followed by a petition to be saved from shame and a declaration of praise in honor of God's steadfast love. At the moment of death, if he is conscious of the entirety of Psalm 31, he is relying on verses 23–24: "Love the Lord, all you his saints. The Lord preserves the faithful but abundantly repays the one who acts haughtily. Be strong, and let your heart take courage, all you who wait for the Lord."

All the while that Psalm 69 is used to anticipate the offer of vinegar to the crucified Jesus, the rest of the psalm poses nearly every spiritual issue related to the crucifixion:

> drowning in tears; vv.1–2

> outnumbered by enemies; v. 4

> "Do not let those who hope in you be put to shame because of me, O Lord God of hosts; do not let those who seek you be dishonored because of me. It is for your sake that I have reproach . . . I have become a stranger to my kindred,

> and alien to my mother's children"; vv. 6–8

> zeal for your house has consumed me; v. 9 (John 2:17)

> object of insults, gossip, and the lyrics of songs; vv.10–12

Then:

> "My prayer is to you, O Lord . . . In the abundance of your steadfast love, answer me. With your faithful help, rescue me . . . let me be delivered from my enemies"; v.13.

> "Do not hide your face from your servant, for I am in distress—make haste to answer me."

By the end of the psalm:

> "Let the oppressed see the reward of the wicked and that the Lord hears the needy and does not despise his own that are in bonds"; vv. 27–33.

How this might relate to the practice of formation is my next task.

1. Formation people can make profitable use of the expression, "the faith of Jesus." The expression opens up the entire issue of Jesus' human nature (Heb 4:14–16; 5:7–10). Richard Hays argues that Jesus is justified by faith just as Abraham was (Gal 3:6, 22; Rom 3:26). The righteousness of God is revealed through the faith of

Jesus, meaning I take it, Jesus trusted in God for vindication, kept himself faithful and was vindicated in the resurrection.[20] God justified Jesus by vindication and in so doing showed that Jesus' faith was not faith in faith but faith in God. Helmut Thielicke argues in a similar fashion, namely, "that I have the new life through and in the fact that Jesus Christ believes, so that here he is thus taken as the prototype of my faith . . . the point where I stand is thus the very point where he so believes."[21] The seminarian/ecclesiastical servant believes with Jesus in the same God.

2. A detailed study of the Psalms used in the composition of the Gospel narratives orients the reader to the formation tradition that was contextual for the isolated verses quoted in the New Testament. To read Psalms like 22, 31, and 69 in their *entirety* is almost reading a transcript of people seeking to move from confusion to confidence. The full psalm is the formational context to pray and behave with Jesus and with those who told his story. But to tell the story of Jesus they had to tell the story that shaped him. Our canon exhibits this narrative coherence.[22]

3. To believe *in* Jesus as well as *with* Jesus puts the believer in touch with marginality. Many of the people Jesus served were the marginalized. By the end of his ministry he was numbered among them. The pain of the marginalized is known in no other way than by letting them teach one what life at edge is like. Hannah and Hagar, Lazarus, and the Syro-Phoenician woman have a story to tell if one allows oneself to hear them. But hearing them created pain, resistance, and anger at them for exercising a claim on one's life; pity, maybe empathy, and perhaps most of all, impotence in being able to do anything.

Two types of marginalities can be identified. One can be called "vulnerability-based marginality." People do not choose it. They have it thrust on them in the form of disabilities, wealth, chronic pain, and a host of other factors. The other is "value-based marginality." People

---

20. Hays, *Faith of Jesus Christ*, 165, 171, 249.

21. Thielicke, *Theological Ethics: Foundations*, 189.

22. Hays, "Paul's Use," 125–27.

"choose" it by choosing a prophetic life that generates opposition and marginalization.[23]

Seminarians and church workers will come to know both forms of marginalization. They can be made instantly vulnerable by disease or disaster, "promotion" or "success." They can make a ministry decision according to values and find themselves alone and maligned. This experience was known in classical theology as the *active obedience* of Jesus, i.e., his active, intentional obedience to the law, and his *passive obedience*, which is what he *underwent* for having actually *undertaken* love of neighbor to the fullest extent. Passive obedience is the hardest since one wants to quit. At this point the seminarian or church worker is called to believe with Jesus that the God who sent Jesus and through Jesus has sent other workers is trustworthy. The faith of Jesus is one's comfort.

IV. The narrative coherence of the two testaments, rooted in the story of one and the same God at work, entails the use of the entire canon of Scripture in formation.

The person who experiences one or both kinds of marginalities described above or who finds obedience to and faith in the God of Israel and Jesus a questionable venture, needs to be taught that the entire canon of Scripture is at one's disposal. My particular reference is to the Psalms of lament and anger. When visited by immobilizing sorrow or intoxicated with anger, the person in formation or in ministry needs to know that such visitations need not be denied or spiritualized. They are real and are not incidental to life as such or to ministry. One can pray one's anger or one's lament in good biblical company.

One example: Brueggemann says that the psalms of anger, generally speaking, have two parts: own it and yield it. Vengeance belongs to God alone.[24] I have had students write anger psalms using this form, together with reading the biblical psalms of anger. This is not a technique. It is a biblical form that frees one to pray angrily one's anger, but pray it nevertheless. There is no way to maintain the relationship except to keep in conversation, at times confronting God, at times conceding yet confessing with Jesus that even though God is the source of our faith, God poses the most challenging questions to faith.

---

23. Keen et al., *Common Fire*, 72–74.
24. Brueggemann, *Praying the Psalms*, 70–71.

V. The model for this spiritual formation is the relation of God to Jesus. God vindicated a faithful but discredited and marginalized person whose faith in God held fast nourished by the story to which and by which he was disciplined.

The faithfulness of God to Jesus is the seminarian's and church worker's margin of strength to persevere in life and in ministry. No such worker has guarantees that he or she will see the fruit of their labor. Moreover, ministry copes with a mystery at its very outset: the very message proclaimed and ministry practiced hardens some and heals other simultaneously. The vocation itself can marginalize the minister by his/her very ministry and message.[25]

The source of perseverance is God who promised that his word would not return void but would accomplish the purpose for which it was sent (Isa 55). But it is not guaranteed that the servant of the word will see the effectiveness either of word or ministry. Resolve to continue is found in this, that the God who vindicated Jesus and Jesus' faith will, in God's time, vindicate the message and ministry carried out by faith and in Jesus' name.

In this manner the spirituality of those who serve may be able to gain some detachment from ministry as a source of ego strength and some differentiation from ministry as a form of identity. Persons in ministry, like Jesus, must await vindication. In the process of waiting it may be learned that one ought not ask God "to bless me and ministry." Rather, following the model suggested, we ask God to vindicate his word and sacraments. In this way some distance may be maintained between the person and his/her vocation so that the vocation does not become all-consuming. In the end it is not the minister's word, it is God's word and God must vindicate God's promises, none of which are subject to human control. The ministry is carried out in the vortex of faith acting in love (Gal 5:6), a faith that as God vindicated Jesus, so God will vindicate the ongoing ministry of word and sacrament.

VI. Lutheran Pietism appropriated Luther's uncompromising insistence on the force of the word order of Galatians 5:6: Faith active in love.[26] Bengel especially appropriated this feature of his heritage to stress the theocentric character of the Christian life. The entire Christian life

25. Juel, "Encountering the Sower," 273–83.

26. See Luther, *Luther's Works* 27:28–31, 333–36.

existed in faith, hope and love.[27] Faith acting in love is the vehicle for the entire Christian faith. [28] Faith is the empowerment and energy of love. Neither faith nor love are self-renewing. But since faith is not faith in faith but in God the subject, faith is subsidized by the one who renews faith by Word and Sacrament. Faith then maintains love's perspective.

Faith in God's will to justify persons through Christ grounds the freedom of the Christian to act for the glory of God and love of neighbor. Faith in God's justifying grace is the source of courage to engage the world for the sake of truth and to give service to one's neighbor without placing ultimate trust in one's capacity to do the task. That capacity may prove to be very limited or the motivation to sustain it may burn out. If one begins this service with love alone, it may sour. If one begins with hope alone, it may be discredited too easily.

Faith does not hesitate to act in love out of concern that one's motives are less than pure or one's commitment less than full strength. If the human concern is that one's love must be right before service to God and neighbor can commence, one will never begin. In a telling exegetical note on Matthew 25:25–26, Bengel says of the one servant who did nothing with the money the master told him to invest but instead buried it out of fear, "*sine amore, sine fiducia* (without love, without confidence)."[29] Distrust of the master truncated the servant's stewardship. The controlling image maintained by the servant was that the master would honor safety over obedience and most of all, trust.

Faith imparts an eschatological dimension to acts of love. Faith can wait for the right time, love wants to make the time now. When love acts in a suffocating manner, it becomes a burden to people in need and gradually deprives them of agency except finally to rebel. In the trying period of waiting the Holy Spirit will bring to our awareness the thing of Christ—not just his words but his confidence in God. When the Holy Spirit bears witness to Jesus Christ it must include God in relation to Christ (John 14–16 and Rom 8:12–30).

Faith waits and knows it has no control over the outcome of the love in which it has acted. Faith learns to be conscientious without being compulsive, compulsiveness being a sign of a lack of faith. In this

27. Bengel, *Neue Testament*, 736.

28. Ibid., "Von der rechten Weise, mit göttlichen Dingen umzugehen," Appendix, section 7, 1000–1001.

29. Bengelii, *Gnomon Novi Testamenti*, 135. Parenthetic translation mine.

way faith knows of a vindication it cannot see and rests its case on the paradigmatic act of God in behalf of Christ, who, on the third day vindicated the work of his son. So the minister relinquishes his/her ministry to God's future, believing with Jesus that God is true to God's word.

In a results oriented culture this is probably bad news. It requires the grave strenuousity of faith to plant seeds and see no plant. But dormant seeds should not be mistaken for dead. They just await "the fire next time" (the words of James Baldwin) as do the seeds of sequoia trees. Ministry and service in league with Jesus Christ requires the grace of relinquishment to remain healthy and hopeful. It means living with God whose ways are not always ours, but whose ways require our service for their accomplishment. Formation in this tradition stresses the faith that acts in love and then, waits—waiting as an intrinsic ministry.

VII. Two brief studies of biblical prayers, one by Moses (value-based marginality: reluctantly he consented to serve his vulnerable people in slavery) and the other by Hannah (a vulnerability-based marginality: infertility), now follow. Both demonstrate *theologia prima* at work trying to traverse the vagaries of primordial thinking.

Moses

In Exodus 32:7–14, the debacle of the golden calf is described. In wrath God says to Moses, "Now let me alone, so that my wrath may burn hot against them and I may consume them; and of you I will make a great nation" (v. 10). Moses once again becomes *defensor fidei* and in authentic fashion turns litigious by a cross-examination of God. In paraphrase: "Why will you grant the Egyptians their point that you brought them out only to kill them?" Second, and surely worth quoting in full: "Turn from your fierce wrath; change your mind and do not bring disaster on your people. Remember Abraham, Isaac and Israel your servants, how you swore to them by your own self, saying to them, 'I will multiply your descendants like the stars of heaven, and all this and that I have promised I will give to your descendants, and they shall inherit it forever'" (vv.12–13).

Samuel Balentine reports that this is the only occurrence in scripture where God is the subject of the sentence "Leave me alone."[30] It is

---

30. Balentine, *Prayer*, 135–39. I also owe my use of "patterned prayer" to Professor Balentine.

a command ignored by Moses and, as I read it, the basis for Moses to take initiative to contravene God's intention to obliterate the people. Moses asks God to take his life and let the people live. The people live and Moses grows introspective about his vocation as the leader of God's people. When the dramatic action has come to an end and Moses has time for some solitude, second thoughts set in. "Now, if I have found favor in your sight, show me your ways so that I might know you and find favor in your sight. Consider too that this nation is your people" (Exod 33:13). God answers, "My presence will go with you and I will give you rest." Moses pushes his point: "If your presence will not go, do not carry us up from here. For how shall it be known that I have found favor in your sight, I and your people, unless you go with us? In this way, we shall be distinct, I and your people from every people on the face of the earth" (vv. 14–16). Moses wants to see God's glory. God says, "I will pass by and while doing so, cover your face with my hand and when I take my hands off, you will see only my back" (vv. 20–23). Fretheim makes the point that when the prophets suffer, part of their vocation is to hold the anguish of God before their people as much as their vocation is to hold the anguish of their people before God.[31] Fretheim concludes that in Moses' prayers the future of Israel is not the only source of such urgent intercession, but also the future of God.[32]

Moses prays two points: "What will the Egyptians say?" and "God, will you go back on your promise?" The former is a forceful question but the latter is the most persuasive—Moses quotes God against God. It is God's word against God's word. This is *theologia prima* at its finest. Like *theologia secunda*, *theologia prima* builds a case and cites sources. It constructs an argument but not primarily *for* God in an apologetic sense but an argument *with* God for the survival of the intercessor's trust and God's reputation. To be sure, there may be a secondary apologetic outcome in that when God does act it adds to God's credibility. But *theologia prima* speaks *to* God and *with* God for the sake of the one who prays and those for whom prayers are offered. The preservation of faithfulness in life is at stake more than the survival of a theological system.

---

31. Fretheim, *Suffering of God*, 104. Fretheim refers to the "divine lament."
32. Ibid., 51.

Hannah

Hanna's situation is instructive for our topic. She is the object of Peninnah's sarcasm as well as the solicitations of Elkanah. On the way to the sanctuary to offer sacrifice he gives her a double portion because "he loved her." Even the solicitousness of Elkanah's question conveys no solace. "Why do you weep? Why do you not eat? Why is your heart sad? Am I not more to you than ten sons?" The last question was the most evocative, the crux of the issue. Hannah's issue is that without sons, who is she, a forbearing husband notwithstanding? Hannah resists any form of solace that evades her truth and she eschews silence as a way of bearing her fate.

The Hannah narrative requires attention to two matters: the incident as a possible "paradigm shift," albeit subtle, and the prayer itself. The liturgical background of this shift is complex, apparently in part due to the varieties of practices that may have preceded the more Deuteronomic standardization and the way women may have participated in these various rites and places, an issue I note but am not competent to assess.[33]

The possible "paradigm shift" happened when Hannah resorted to silent prayer in the sanctuary yet moved her lips. Gerald Sheppard comments about Eli's puzzle over Hannah's prayer practice: "The tradition assumes that Eli's inability to overhear the prayer is exceptional rather than normal. As in the case of Job, prayers were not considered in general in the Old Testament to be secretive, silent, or private exercises. The capacity of a prayer to be overheard is a characteristic rather than an incidental feature of it."[34]

The possible trajectory of this shift has been drawn out by two other contemporary scholars. The Hebraist Marcia Falk, having noted this innovation, argues that the Hannah narrative will later become the model for "the prayer of the heart." She further asserts that Hannah's protest to Eli that she was not drunk and wanted to be heard "became the basis for a later rabbinic ruling that one must not let a false charge to oneself go uncorrected—one must not be apathetic in defense of oneself" (the source she cites is the Babylonian Talmud, tractate *Berakhot* 31b.)[35]

---

33. Lapsley, "Pouring Out," 8–15.
34. Sheppard, "Enemies," 98–99.
35. Falk, "Reflections," 98–99.

Cynthia Ozick argues in a similar way.[36] Hanna lived before the time the House of the Lord had become a House of Prayer. In doing so, Ozick avers a new understanding of God: God is not only the commander of events but also the listener to the small voice, a voice capable despite its weakness to influence an event (the opening of her womb).

Given that Hannah was of questionable value because of her closed womb and thus reduced to instrumentality (reproductive function), when Hannah mustered the *chutzpah* to enter the sanctuary and confront the Almighty using her own words, Ozick says, "instrinsicness declares itself against instrumentality."[37]

The content of Hannah's prayer (1 Sam 1:10–11) is strikingly similar to the words of Exodus 2:23–24. Hannah: "O Lord of hosts, if only you will *look upon* the misery of your servant, and *remember* me, and *not forget* your servant, but will give to your servant a child, then . . . ." Exodus: "The Israelites groaned under their slavery and cried out. Out of their slavery their cry for help rose up to God. God *heard* their groaning and God *remembered* his covenant with Abraham, Isaac, and Jacob. God *looked* upon Israel and God *took notice* of them" (emphasis added). If so, Hannah forged a combination of patterned prayer and personal prayer. Her prayer, having some of the language of a *credo*, was her petition but was based on a history. Hannah forms an argument from history for a new history in which she would be the chief beneficiary of this new exodus. She prayed the story even as the story prayed her. Hannah was practicing *theologia prima*, quoting its sources and identifying her "innovative" act as perfectly in line with her ancestors who prayed their faith that God heard, looked, took notice, and remembered his covenant with the ancestors.

Previously in this prayer I had noted Fretheim's observation that Moses, by praying, participated in the anguish of God as much as he presented the anguish of the people before God. In a somewhat analogous fashion Ronald Wallace suggests a similar vocation for Hannah. Averring that she was troubled by the sanctuary corruption as reflected in the behavior of Eli's sons, she found a reason to reorient the anguish over her childlessness. If she had a child who became a prophet like Moses, he could rebuke corruption and properly set forth God's word. Wallace, taking note that the custom of the day prohibited such a role

36. Ozick, "Hannah and Elkanah," 89.
37. Ibid., 90.

to her, argues that in praying for a son she was doing so vicariously as if in the indirect way of motherhood she too was entering into conflict with God's opponents and becoming prophetic. In so doing she knew the anguish of a prophet. Living with God meant women's understanding of God's anguish.[38]

But the system has problems with too many Hannah's around. In trying to say too much, offering too many explanations based on the axioms of the system, it turns out in the end to be too axiomatic and at least perceptibly, contradictory. Sometimes *theologia secunda* ends up serving the system rather that the people who are trying to believe or the God who is to be believed.

Hannah's *theologia prima* was short on axioms but long on anticipation that vindication was a prayable issue. Her primordial encounter with God, like that of Moses, did not render her speechless. If anything, it made speech a necessity. Is prayer perhaps God's own speech back to God in a human voice?

VIII. A pedagogical move is suggested by Moltmann: "There can be no theology 'after Auschwitz' which does not take up the theology in Auschwitz, i.e., the prayers and cries of the victims."[39] I am listing five works that pray a theology "in" some situation. Readers of these texts will notice an intertestamental as well as intratestamental use of texts, characters, and stories as a way of praying the story to which and by which one is disciplined as well as allowing the story to pray through the intercessor. Primordial theological thinking is doing its theological work in the only method it knows—prayer— but it is prayer rooted in sources and relying on the canonical coherence of the narratives used. Two of my five examples are liturgical.

> *Liturgies on the Holocaust: An Interfaith Anthology*, edited by Marcia Sachs Littell
>
> *Conversations with God: Two Centuries of Prayers by African Americans*, edited with introduction by James Melvin Washington
>
> Erhard S. Gerstenberger, "Singing a New Song: On Old Testament and Latin American Psalmody"

38. Wallace, *Hannah's Prayer*, 6–8.
39. Moltmann, *History*, 29.

Stephen P. McCutchen, "Framing Our Pain: The Psalms in Worship," *The Christian Ministry*.[40]

Rosemary Radford Ruether, *Women-Church: Theology and Practice of Feminist Liturgical Communities*, pp. 153–58.[41]

CONCLUSION

No matter the marginalizations in life, whether vulnerability-based or values-based, they cannot be put on hold, whether in seminary or in ministry. But such marginalization need not put life on hold. Yet while marginalizations may never be fully remediated, they can be related to the larger perspective of the canonical text, namely, that God is to be trusted. At times one must take another's word for it. Prayer thus is always in company.

God can be lived with, but not easily. A grave strenuousity of faith is required to do primordial thinking where thinking and praying seem to merge. When the primordial thinker is tempted to quit thinking, it is probably not that the questions are too hard but that the thinker-pray-er is afraid to pray his or her thoughts about God to God. But the fearful can be fortified by the canonical narrative that is populated with persons who can quote God to God, not to blaspheme but to trust more deeply. When one's imaging systems preclude honest prayer, let the narratives embolden and equip one to pray biblically so that the faith in the God of Abraham, Moses, Hannah, and Jesus is allowed to mature in the way it acts in love. If the faith is not allowed to mature, it will not act.

40. Pastor McCutchen illustrates a narrative and canonical coherence in liturgical use by suggesting Psalms 42 and 43 to parents of critically ill children; Psalm 39 and the story of St. Peter's denial as coordinates in the case of suicide; and lastly Psalm 88 and 2 Samuel 13:1–22 (the rape of Tamar) as a way of dealing with rape and abuse homiletically.

41. Ruether reproduces a rite of healing for victims of domestic violence contextualized in the midst of friends that is a narrative paraphrase of Psalm 22. The rite she reproduces is taken from Del Martin, *Battered Wives* (San Francisco: Glide, 1976), 1–5.

2

Jesus and His Baptismal Maturation

Living with God While Living for God

THE RITE OF ORDINATION in the Evangelical Covenant Church begins with renewal of the candidate's baptism. It is a way of saying that at the time of the candidate's investiture in the office of the ministry the transcendental grounding of the entire enterprise is in need of restatement. Baptism has a fullness to it that, like marriage, remains future to the public rite. Its gifts and graces, its calling and vocation call for a continual process of maturation. One never knows the cost of one's discipleship until in some life situation, when public witness is called for, the bill comes due. When such occasions happen, the person is growing into his or her baptism. Baptismal maturity is the name for such obedient faithfulness.

The idea of baptismal maturity came to me from reading Professor Clinton Morrison's exegetical study, "Baptism and Maturity."[1] Morrison's intriguing study of New Testament expressions such as "little ones," "little children," and "newborn babes" shows their setting in baptismal contexts, all suggesting the vulnerability of new born disciples and immature converts. Thus these terms suggest congregational *protection* for both the literal children and the metaphoric use for new converts. He also shows how such words had a *polemical* function in guarding against the false sense of spiritual elitism since all were to turn and become as

1. Morrison, "Baptism and Maturity."

34

little children. Finally, Morrison shows the *pastoral* dimension of such expressions since the "little ones" are to be weaned gradually from the "milk" of the word to the "meat" of the word.[2]

Not only Jesus but also St. Paul employed similar language in speaking of his pastoral work. To the Galatians he was a woman in travail (Gal 4:19); to the Thessalonians, a nurse (1 Thess 2:7f); and a paternal figure in 1 Corinthians 4:14f. Each of these metaphors suggests that the recipients of St. Paul's ministrations were in some crucial stage of a maturation process.

Morrison brings his discussion to a startling premise: all baptisms in the New Testament were the baptism of little children regardless of age. Why? Presumably none were mature enough to know the outcome of their act until the bill came due, until the time came for the truth to come out, for life to match words. As Morrison answers, "The New Testament commands that one turn and become as a child and does not ask, 'Are you yet old enough?'"[3] The upshot of this line of reflection is that no candidate for baptism is "old enough," i.e., mature enough to know just exactly what is being promised until the occasion arises. What about Jesus who himself requested baptism?

The first insight into the maturation of Jesus can be found in Luke's cryptic words, "And Jesus increased wisdom and in years and in divine and human favor" (Luke 2:52). The text leaves no doubt that at twelve he could hold his own in debate with religious authorities. What the text leaves unsaid is how parent-child matters were negotiated. This is especially pertinent in this text since at a festival in Jerusalem Jesus takes off for three days, noticed missing at the time to return home. It's every parent's nightmare. What else to say but, "Child, why have you treated us this way?" Whatever made up that conversation it was part of the maturation process for Jesus and his parents.

Textual silence reigns over the years between the temple debate and the baptism. As I envision Luke's description (3:10–17), Jesus is lined up along the riverbank with a cross-section of the population all involved in some way or another with a public life in need of repentance. According to Matthew, even the religious establishment is among the crowd and in this context John spots his relative Jesus and denies wanting any role in his baptism. Instead, John asks Jesus to baptize him. Jesus refuses and

2. Ibid., 395–99.
3. Ibid., 400.

says he has to be baptized in order to fulfill all righteousness (Matt 3:15; cf. vv. 7–17). The point needs to be made: Jesus will not step out of the crowd requesting baptism. The text leaves the impression that he wills to be numbered among them and will bear the reputation later as being one of them.

After his baptism an extraordinary event happens. A voice from heaven says, "This is my Son, the Beloved with whom I am well pleased." As witness, the Holy Spirit descends like a dove. Word and sign, voice and visibility mark out the uniqueness of this event and the person who is its center. But God always speaks with word and sign: recall the rainbow to Noah and the promise never to destroy the earth with a flood.

The baptismal narratives in the Gospels are classic examples of what was called in the first chapter, narrative coherence. They are neither freestanding texts nor isolated verses but rather assemble a vast array of Old Testament texts and stories that together are the story Jesus lived with, lived out of, lived into and in the end, to which Jesus contributed. William Manson has an instructive word as to how these stories function as a history: "When we today think of *history*, we think of it as a series or stream of events, in which the earlier are always dropping behind the horizon as the new events come on. But in the Bible *time* is not a stream but a structure. It is a structure of Divine acts in which all the parts are held together."[4]

As I read Manson, *time* is a structure in the making. The Jesus story is part of the cohering narrative of the one and same God who brought Israel out of Egypt and Jesus out of the tomb and who promises to do another Exodus-Resurrection of God's people now held in tombs, urns, and unmarked burial plots. What goes on in the time between the times is in some way connected with the final Exodus. Somewhere in my memory I recall Oscar Cullmann having written that every miracle Jesus performed was a partial resurrection: a feeding miracle redeems from starvation, a healing miracle from death, an exorcism redeems a personality from dissolution—all in one way or another showing that death had an announced opponent, a relentless adversary who fought death at every level: physical, psychological, and spiritual. But to tell this story the evangelists did not invent new words or categories as much as they took the time structure given chaos–creation; bondage–exodus; exile–return and showed how these events or even paradigms held true

4. Manson, *Jesus and the Christian*, 36.

for the Jesus story.[5] As the evangelists told it, Jesus lived out of, with and into this structure. From this history hope gained currency, particularly for Jesus and so no one could say his baptismal maturity did not need to come to full expression.

Saint Matthew in particular prefaces the telling of the Jesus story and its place in the "time structure" with a telling line. Dale Allison, a Matthean scholar of note, translates 1:1: "The book of Genesis of Jesus Christ son of David son of Abraham." He shows the immediate connection with the Septuagint's version of Genesis 2:4, "This is the book of genesis of heaven and earth . . ." and Genesis 5:1, "This is the book of genesis of human beings."[6] How different a beginning than the more traditional rendering of the genealogy or ancestry of Jesus Christ![7] Is St. Matthew announcing something new, so new that only the radicality of the creation story can show that God is the chief actor in the story? This is especially so when one reads the list of Jesus' ancestors, a list of people of mixed bloodlines and mixed morals. Yet in this paradox one finds the gospel in miniature: hidden in this list of disqualified ones is the Qualified One. God's Chosen One will appear under some other identity, most notably, God in flesh among very fleshly people.[8] It is not surprising then that he is awaiting his turn for baptism standing among such an odd collection of people seeking repentance.

The evangelists are unanimous in the appearance of a dove. Is it not a recollection of the Noah flood story where the dove sent out by Noah does not return from the third time sent out? The waters have receded. The time to exodus the ark has come. A new time for humans has come, namely, to begin anew as the first family of a renewed humanity. St. Peter Chrysologus, bishop of Ravenna in the fifth century, and said that God had shut "into one ark the seedling creatures of the whole new world, that the love of fellowship may banish the fear characteristic of bondage, and a common love preserve what a common toil had saved."[9] So is the Noah story being recalled at Jesus' baptism and is he the "seedling of a

5. Wright, *Jesus and the Victory*, 125–33, 538–39, and part 3. This massive book is an elaboration of these motifs.

6. Allison, *Studies in Matthew*, 157–62.

7. Hooker, "Beginning," 27–28. Morna Hooker likewise shows that the issues raised by Alison are indeed intrinsic to Matthew's presentation of the gospel.

8. See, for example, Sakenfeld, "Tamar, Rehab, Ruth," 21–31.

9. Chrysologus, *Selected Sermons*, 244.

new creation?" As Manson argued, the writers of the Gospels knew how to use history as a "time structure." Thus the time of Jesus, like the time of Noah, like the time of Genesis, was a time to begin new, but accompanied both by death and new life. The old creation was still retained and was the location of God's continued redemptive staging operation. God never let loose of creation. God was doing a new thing, the end of which awaited the Chosen One, now baptized, to let the story both mature in him and mature him.

At his baptism Jesus heard a voice declaring him a *beloved son* and at the transfiguration the same voice speaks of him as the *chosen one* and adds some new words: "Listen to him." Manson writes that this reference to sonship has at least four Old Testament roots: Adam, created in the image of God; the calling of Israel at the Exodus, "Israel is my Son, my first born; let my Son go that He may serve me" (Exod 4:22–23); the royal enthronement text, "The Lord has said to me, 'Thou art my Son'" (Pss 2:7); and lastly Isaiah 42, where the investiture of the Spirit is sent upon the chosen servant.[10]

The use of Isaiah 42 in both the stories of Jesus' baptism and transfiguration suggests much more than the use of about three to five words. Read the text as the vocation of the Chosen One. In part it reads: he will bring forth justice to the nations; he will conduct ministry so as not to snuff out dimly burning wicks nor will he faint or grow weary until he has established justice in the earth (vv. 1–4 in part). This, I take it, is what the evangelists mean when they say that he will fulfill all righteousness. Is that not why in Luke 4, when day one, so to speak, of Jesus' ministry begins, the agenda is set again by Isaiah 58 and 61? Anointed by the Spirit (Luke 4 restates the investiture of the Spirit first given at baptism), Jesus is now entering an Isaianic vocation, that is, prophets take on injustice and so the "time structure" once again makes space for a new prophet but clearly in continuity with God's previous work. Something new is in the making. Water, dove, and voice say so. But water, dove, and voice have a history. That is what makes them both credible and recognizable to Jesus, the Gospel writers, and to later hearers and readers.

Interwoven between the lines of the story I have told ever so sketchily is the complex issue of identity description. I find Princeton sociologist Robert Wuthnow's distinction between an *ascribed* (or conferred)

---

10. Manson, *Jesus and the Christian*, 37–38.

identity and an *achieved* identity a perceptive differentiation.[11] A king for example, did not *achieve* royal status. The title and role are ascribed due to bloodlines and a public coronation. Abraham Lincoln was *ascribed* the marker identity of president by the peoples' vote and constitutional provision for an office of president, but he *achieved* the identity of the great emancipator by what he accomplished.

Jesus received his religious identity in his circumcision. In this act he inherited all the promises made to Abraham. He was initiated into the story of this *ascribed* identity, "child of Abraham," as his family celebrated the annual round of feasts. When identity is ascribed, not achieved, it is appropriated communally by hearing and repeating the story, not only liturgically and ritually but also by personal testimony as people say, "Here is where Abraham's God helped me."

This assumes that one will permit two strands of the story equal play in one's life: the core witness (the testimony to God's victorious assistance such as the exodus, commemorated in Deuteronomy 26:5–11, Isaiah 40, Psalms 107, 140; and the resurrection in 1 Corinthians 15, 2 Corinthians 14–16) and the counter testimony (the psalms of lament, anger, the disquieting stories of rape such as Tamar, the life of Job, infertility such as Hannah or banishment such as Hagar).[12] It will be recalled that in the Forward the structured, reliable core testimony was called the "mythic" while the disorienting, disillusioning aspects of the life of faith was termed the "parabolic." When the two strands are allowed their integrity one can more truly find a place in the story, especially when one's story is a repeat of those whose testimony is anything but triumphant. When Jesus' ascribed identity was given him in circumcision he was being equipped with core witness and counter testimony, both of which the New Testament says he used during his maturing into the accompanying *ascribed identities* given at baptism (my Beloved) and at transfiguration (my Chosen).

Can one speak legitimately of Jesus maturing in his baptism? I know such a thought sounds ridiculous if not blasphemous. But let us let the Bible help us. Jesus' maturation as a person has already been referenced (Luke 2:52). The concern here is his baptismal vocation: to fulfill all righteousness. A future element is implied: something is to be fulfilled, a fulfilling that awaits his obedience. Helped by texts in Hebrews

11. Wuthnow, *Christianity*, 185–91, cf. 42–45.

12. Brueggemann, *Theology*, parts 1 and 2 as listed in the table of contents.

2:10 and 5:8–9 we come to know that he learned obedience through what he suffered and as the text says, was perfected by such suffering. Consequently Jesus knew something about a learned obedience, but not a photograph of each solution before he engaged it. If not so, why would Hebrews 2:17–18 and 4:14–15 tell us that he would be tempted in every way yet without sin and that he lifted up his soul with loud cries (Heb 5:7) if not because of the cost of baptismal maturity, the cost of fulfilling all righteousness? Is not Gethsemane the culmination of his baptismal fidelity—"what shall I say, 'Save me from this hour'"? And then his deepest pain: "Let this cup pass from me." All along he was being shaped by and into the identity of the "Chosen One." With every sense of propriety I think one can speak of the maturation of Jesus' baptismal identity.

So it was in concrete incidents. Think of Jesus' encounters. John 4 describes a conversation with a Samaritan woman, herself unable to visit the well in the morning with her peers because of her reputation. Jesus, a Jew, asks for a drink. Think of it: a Jew dependent on a Samaritan. A conversation follows that gets at her reputation. The text says she went back to her village and invited her acquaintances to come hear a man who told her all she ever did. I note that nowhere in the text does it even hint, despite her growing awareness of the person of her conversation partner, *that she felt told off*. A lesson in pastoral care: the truth can be gotten at without making the person anymore the victim of their self-hatred than they already are. Baptismal maturity takes one across boundaries—ethnic, religious, and moral. That's what it means to be chosen: Go there. Be there. It would become the story of the Acts of the Apostles. This all started with the Chosen One being dependent on a Samaritan woman. Maturation of baptism?

Or think about the Syro-Phonecian woman (Mark 7:24–30). This Gentile had a daughter who was ill and begged healing of Jesus. Jesus said, "Let the children be fed first, for it is not fair to take the children's food and throw it to the dogs." Then came a response like out of left field: "Sir, even the dogs under the table eat the children's crumbs." Once again chosen to be where boundaries seemed to say "off limits." Was this another moment of growing into the ascribed identity: baptized and chosen? Are not these examples of a "genesis," a new creation taking shape, the time of the dove for the face of the earth? He even healed the child of a Roman centurion, granting divine favor to a captor of Israel. With this act an eschatological feature comes forth with a vengeance: at the consummation Abraham and Sarah will host the centurion at the great messianic feast—and if the centurion, who else? This one act of healing was a taste of the new creation. In one of his writings, Ernst Käsemann says that the modern missionary movement did not begin with the great commission but with Jesus' statement, "Eat what is set before you." That undid Leviticus 11 and the dietary boundary representing a new time zone in the time structure of the story. It was a time as radical as the first day of creation or the day after the flood had subsided.

Among his own people it was to be no different. He ate at the home of tax collectors and called one of them, Matthew, to be his disciple. He touched lepers in the process of healing them. Prostitutes found that he would not summarily dismiss them with stinging words of ridicule and condemnation. Children, often the overlooked segment of society, became the focal point of his sermons. He spoke of giving feasts for the maimed, the lame, the blind, and other outcasts and of making such the most honored of guests.

A popular moniker for this increasingly disillusioning Jesus was "a glutton, a wine-bibber, and a sinner." This moniker is a quotation from Deuteronomy 21:20, where it describes a rebellious son who has brought nothing but shame on his family and whose punishment was death by stoning. Jesus' *ascribed identity*—chosen one—the repository of so many hopes and expectations for deliverance from captivity to a foreign power came into increased conflict with his *achieved identity*—friend of sinners and outcasts—and one who disregards the people's hopes.

At the end of his life Jesus is asked by James and John to do for them whatever they ask. What did they want? For one to sit on his right hand and the other on his left in the kingdom. Jesus posed a baptismal question: "Are you able to drink the cup that I drink or be baptized with the baptism I am baptized with?" Their answer was straightforward: "We are able." Jesus continued: "The cup that I drink you will drink; and the baptism with which I am baptized you will be baptized . . ." (Mark 10: 35–39). But he hands out no advanced seating assignments, only a hint at their coming baptismal maturation.

The enterprise of the Chosen One comes to an end on a cross, the most despicable form of death, the form reserved for the criminals and traitors. In this context the piety of Jesus is disclosed in some detail. When he prays it is to Abraham's God, Moses' God, his mother's and father's God and, to him, the One who had called him "My Chosen."

So when he prayed he used other people's prayers, often drawn from the counter testimony, maybe for two reasons: he had come to the end of his own words in the experience of loss and abandonment (including God's) and to pray the Psalms meant not only petitioning but also confessing a faith (the core witness) that his ancestors had used. So one reads carefully the texts of Psalms 22, noting how like prayers in distress it is: verse 1 accuses God of forsaking, verse 3 acclaims God as holy. Two contradictory inclinations vie for dominance in the soul. Read on and note how the "yet" functions along with "but," just the way we negotiate our way through life.

Jesus also prays Psalm 31 as a form of committal. Note how theocentric it is. Be mindful also of the pain of public scorn and of dread even to those thought to be close. To the very end the prayer is to be kept from shame. In dying Jesus prays for those who did him in, denied him, sold him, and killed him as the chosen and who had identified with him. But the cross event looked like anything but vindication, not like anything had been fulfilled. Rather it looked as though all had come apart at the seams. Nothing here resembled Genesis 1–2. It comes across more like the devastation of Genesis 9 (flood) and 11 (tower of Babel). The whole thing looked old and as if nothing had changed. Bloodshed was routine. Betrayal was expedient. Denial was safer. The days of Noah were alive and well. Hawks, not doves, were flying.

But then the women associates of Jesus said that on the first day of the week they had seen the Lord. He was not in the tomb. Their witness has become immortalized in the acclamation "He is risen." But the New Testament is not content with that. It leaves God out of the picture and his fidelity to Jesus in question, which in turn puts the confidence of each Christian in some kind of jeopardy. So the preaching of Acts and the theological statements of the Epistles are nearly unanimous that Jesus did not rise from the dead but that God raised him (see Acts 2:23–29; 2:36; 3:15; 5:30–31; Rom 1:1–5; 8:11; Gal 1:1; Phil 2:5–11; and 1 Cor 6:41 among others). The raising of Jesus from the dead is once again God's act of public identification with this discredited man from Nazareth, the repository of so many hopes, the terminus of so many expectations, and the source of such a sense of betrayal. God raised him and identified with this crucified one as his Chosen One. Everything Jesus did, every person with whom he identified, every word he spoke was the fulfilling of all righteousness and played some part in the baptismal maturation of Jesus. In the end it was God who was the sponsor of Jesus of Nazareth.

A brief reprise: At his circumcision Jesus was ascribed his religious identity. At his baptism a vocational identity was ascribed to him. At his transfiguration his baptismal identity was reaffirmed with the voice from heaven repeating virtually the identical words spoken at baptism. This was the final equipping to face the cross. The voice identified with the Beloved, Chosen Son despite the growing public disaffection and disillusionment. This same voice would call him back to life and out of the tomb.

For those of us in vocational ministry, I will contend it is the God-Jesus relation that is the basic structure for our vocational spirituality. It is incumbent upon us to speak, not only of our baptismal maturity but also of our ordinational maturity. Such maturity is best fostered by the exemplar of the God-Jesus relation: although there was a long silence before Easter and the public vindication with the assurance of divine identification, God in God's time acts. So for us in vocational ministry: God will be faithful to God's word. The resurrection of Jesus Christ is our guarantee, even though Holy Saturday can be along time.

3

Laying On of Hands

I HAVE A SUSPICION THAT St. Augustine was a virtual mind reader of those of us who occupy the pastoral office:

> The day I became a bishop, a burden was laid on my shoulders for which it will be no easy task to render account. The honors I receive are for me an ever-present cause of uneasiness. Indeed, it terrifies me to think that I could take more pleasure in the honor attached to my office, which ought to be its fruit. This is why being set above you fills me with alarm, whereas being with you gives me comfort. Danger lies in the first; salvation in the second.
>
> By finding my chief joy therefore in redemption, which I share with you, and not in my office, which has placed me over you, I shall the more truly be your servant; and so not only fulfill the Lord's command, but also show myself not ungrateful to him for making me your fellow servant. For my Redeemer has a claim on my love, and I do not forget how he questioned Peter, and asked, 'Do you love me, Peter? Then feed my sheep.' He asked this one, then again and then a third time. He inquired about his love, and then gave him work to do; for the greater one's love is, the easier is the work![1]

You may need to substitute "pastor" or another equivalent word. Reread the text using the word appropriate to your vocational location. Be mindful that twice St. Augustine speaks both of his *position* of entrusted authority *and* of his *place* alongside the people. Do you feel endangered by your office? Or that the abuse of the office of the ministry is a danger to the congregation? Is it not also necessary to think of pastoral

---

1. Augustine, *Sermon 340*, 1561–62.

abuse in at least two ways: the arrogant abuse of authority, knowledge, and power, and/or the abuse fostered by passivity, neglect, and indifference? To which temptation are you most vulnerable?

Arrogance and abdication of position are abuses of power. I am submitting a text from John Esau, an Anabaptist, whose reflection on the empowering nature of office may assist those who are reluctant to engage their ministry with a full wealth of conviction.[2] These are the intimidated ones, often silenced and immobilized by abdication. The original issue posed to Mr. Esau was how any young pastor could have any significant role in ministering to those older than him/herself. Mr. Esau responded by laying out the implied notion:

> Life experience only empowers one to minister to one's equal in age or younger. As long as ministry depends solely upon the person and their experience, such limitations might be understood. What is not understood in these questions is the empowering nature of the office that both enables and demands that we serve in a representational role that transcends what age we are or what we have experienced in life.
>
> Most people have at times the added strength of an office to carry out tasks that they are expected to perform, knowing that they did this not only because of their giftedness, but because others carried expectations and role perceptions for them. When we function within clearly defined roles to which others have called us, we know ourselves to be strengthened by the community we serve.[3]

Ezekiel 34:1–10 is a classic text on abdication. Indifference to one's people could hardly be described in more graphic terms. The tragedy in this case is that the office holder will behave as if he or she has been installed in no office. Indifference in this instance is about as radical a species of denial as one can find. It is pretense of office without the performance of office.

Do you think of your office as empowering? Think of the *privilege of access* you have: to ICU units, to hospitals, prisons, to houses and families, to individuals with whom you initiate conversations. When giving counsel one can say, "Your situation has appeared before . . . there's a story like it in scripture or in church history or in biography." Your of-

---

2. I owe the last four words to the subtitle of a book written by Diogenes Allen: *Christian Belief in a Postmodern World: The Full Wealth of Conviction.*

3. Esau, *Understanding*, 16.

fice, for which you prepared to occupy, carries with it a certain enabling power. You do know of access to resources of various kinds for various needs and your office does give you a certain official reason to call and be listened to by the appropriate authorities.

As I see it, ascribed identity is what ordination bestows. In St. Augustine's terms, it can be turned into an office of abusive power. In terms represented by Mr. Esau it can be an enabling power. One of the ways I am helped in my maturation process is this way. When I put on my purple gown and PhD hood from Northwestern University I have the *achieved* identity of "doctor." It was earned and cannot be withdrawn no matter how dissolute a life I live. When I put on my alb and stole, the symbol of ordination, I am reminded of an *ascribed* identity. I neither earned nor merited ordination. I earned the appropriate theology degree. But the church that ordained me can revoke my ordination and remove my stole. The church, not I, is the custodian of my ordination.

The "power" attached therefore to the office of the ministry is derivative and the authority is contingent on my stewardship of the trust of office. Either abuse or abdication is grounds for dismissal or discipline. St. Augustine's terror was in forgetfulness of the ascribed and contingent character of his privilege to be in office, which turns occupants of the office into self-appointed authorities whose sense of ministerial identity has lost its ascribed character and has embraced an achieved character. Such persons inevitably seem to be on a career track more than living out a vocation. The mentality of the achieved identity can afford little room for critical appraisal by others because it is received in such a personal way. No distance exists between the occupant of the office and the office. Even the office itself, its history and tradition, can offer little to such persons except to feed the sense of authoritarianism, not withstanding that the literature offers counsel in depth about the dangers so well articulated by St. Augustine.

Mr. Esau's trust in the office is deeply aware of the contingent and derivative character of the ascribed authority of the occupant. The authority is ascribed and the power in part derived from the laying on of hands. For my part, the ritual act carries the trust, authorizing, and consent of centuries of persons in office. More immediately, for the Evangelical Covenant Church, the ordaining body of the author, the authorization and consent of the denomination flows through the hands of the Board of Ordered Ministry, those already in office, on the heads of ordinands to say nothing of the confirmation by the Holy Spirit that such persons are in place, entrusted with ministry of Word and Sacrament. In this sense the office "makes up" for lack of experience as long as the occupant does not pretend to know more than he or she knows.[4] Our competence is in the ministry of Word and Sacrament, the intent and extent of our ministry. But, as will be noted in a later chapter, it is our person present to other persons in life settings that exceeds in value most anything else a pastor does. This is not the resident expert, Mr. Fix It, but a priest and prophet of the Triune God whose ascribed identity is the authorization to serve Word and Sacrament and by so doing to bear rule in the spirit of Christ. Let the authorization of the ordination service be one's freedom and competence. And be reminded that the final authorization and validation of the ministry of Word and Sacrament is the resurrection, the witness to the God who is true to his promise. That makes ministry possible.

Thus pastoral office holders are persons with authority but under authority. Helmut Thielicke's reflections on power provide cogent language for a more theoretical conceptuality. Persons in leadership positions are continually negotiating the territory between autonomy and authority.[5] No one likes to be a puppet. Persons are subjects who have ideas, talents, creativity, varying degrees of vision for the future, varying skills in leadership, to say nothing of ambitions, personality types, and levels of physical prowess. This can feed an autonomy that functions out of a sense of self-authorization and, in persons psychologically immature, self-actualization.

Authority, says Thielicke, is to be distinguished from force.[6] Tyranny treats others as objects with no autonomy; authority treats others as subjects respecting an appropriate sense of autonomy. Autonomy and authority are enabled to work in a joint manner by a "third thing," an agreed-to document such as the Constitution or the Bible to which a group looks for direction and whose authority it receives. Meetings, for example, are workable because parliamentary procedure negotiates between autonomy (self-willed individualism) and authority (control by

---

4. See Jenson, *Visible Words*, ch. 18; and Gritsch and Jenson, *Lutheranism*, ch. 8, but especially pp. 116–21.

5. Thielicke, *Theological Ethics*, 180–89.

6. Ibid., 186.

the few). Parliamentary procedure is the "third thing," whose role it is to give as much public access to the process as possible.[7]

Thielicke's notion of "advance credit" is a major insight.[8] When it comes to leadership, trust granted by an autonomous person to another is the "advance credit" that sustains authority. But securing this "advance credit" is the willingness of all parties to be subject to the "third thing." For the clergy of the Covenant Church the "third thing" includes the Bible, the Constitution of the Evangelical Covenant Church, the Rules of the Board of the Ordered Ministry and Guidelines for Covenant Ministers. Other church traditions will cite a Book of Discipline, a Book of Confessions, a Book of Order, or Book of Canon Law. Confidence arises when it is clear that the one in authority and the ones served are governed by the same "third thing." Living with and under the "third thing" testifies to the ascribed identity that is a trust and a vocation, never a career and an achievement. It will be forever the case that an "ordinational maturity" is never fully achieved, as situations will arise tempting one to an autonomy that seeks the quick fix or efficient method of authoritarianism as the path of choice. At the same time, situations will tempt others to capitulate saying, "What's the use? Things will never change." Abuse and abdication are perversions of an autonomy that violates the credit extended, testing to the limit the trust that people place in their leaders.

Ordinational maturity exceeds the boundary issues of the place and power of office. "Advance credit" has something to do with the maintenance of credibility as it is carried out in the practice or avoidance of ministry. Extended credit by any person seeking pastoral care assumes in some way the competence of the practitioner of ministry. Competence goes in two directions. On the one hand, the practitioner knows his or her technical limits and when and to whom a referral needs to be made. I presume we all know the delicacy of this matter: every safeguard needs to be in place so that the one referred does not sense abandonment. On the other hand, the practitioner of ministry requires enough spiritual discernment and integrity to name resistances to certain persons or issues that would interfere with the practitioner's intention to minister in a fashion consonant with the vows of their ordinational discipline and with accessibility to the person seeking help. It may be that the prac-

7. Ibid., 180, 187, 203.

8. Ibid., 185.

titioner would be well served by spiritual direction in order to be able to name such resistances, which were presented in their more or less traditional forms in chapter 1. In seeking neither to abuse nor abdicate one's office, is it not possible to speak truthfully with persons in such a way that convictions can be spoken without contempt? That honest difference can be acknowledged and the conditions for helpfulness be assessed in a fashion that does not need to terminate relationships? It is ironic but true that people can be served even when differences require admission. Truth telling can be done self-righteously, almost as an act of power. Or it can be done as St. Paul says, "Speaking the truth in love, we must grow up in every way into him who is head, even Christ . . ." (Eph 4:15). Truth telling is not motivationally neutral. When spoken by any one in pastoral office it is power laden and authority driven. Truth telling can also be grace filled and hope suggestive. The former, when abused, has a way of canceling the credit extended, the latter confirms that it was a risk well taken.

Ordinational maturity includes a wide range of opportune moments. Just how wide the range of involvement may be is described this way in the Ethical Principles for Covenant Ministers: "We offer pastoral care to anyone regardless of race, gender, creed, ethnic origin, socio-economic status or sexual orientation."[9] How such a range comes to our attention may be as surprising to us as to Jesus: "While he was teaching . . . just then some men came carrying a paralyzed man on his bed . . ." (Luke 5:17–18). While teaching . . . just then "after this he went out and saw a tax collector named Levi and said, 'Follow me'" (5:27). "On one occasion he was going to the house of a Pharisee to eat a meal on the Sabbath. They were watching him closely. Just then, in front of him, there was a man who had epilepsy . . . Jesus took him and healed him" (14:1–2, 4). My choice of texts is enough to show that it still goes on: on the way to . . . we see . . . while preparing a sermon, a call comes. In the community, where one lives, an issue, an incident arises for pastoral attention. One can put it this way: ordinational maturity relates to ministry that is both intentional (what we plan to do) and incidental (what we don't plan but what requires care). The Ethical Guidelines for Pastors in Covenant churches can be inclusive of all sorts of persons

9. Specific guidelines for the pastoral practice and polity of the clergy of the Evangelical Covenant Church may be obtained from the Office of the Ordered Ministry at http://www.covchurch.org/ministry.

much like those with whom Jesus identified in his baptism to fulfill all righteousness. With the advent of his identification with such a variety of persons, as the Gospel describes, there is also the "genesis" for them of a new creation and a chance to hear words similar to what Jesus heard at this baptism: "My Chosen." Think of the ministry as a gift to persons in need when we in pastoral office choose to identify with them. But having chosen to fulfill a ministry we in office need to be prepared for a process of ordinational maturation. After all, someone is extending credit to us and it is incumbent on us in ministry to demonstrate that we are a trustworthy risk. Three scenarios:

The first instance is perhaps speculative but not entirely. If the bird flue or H1N1 pandemic hit where one serves, has thought been given to how one might respond with ordinational maturity? I suppose the first thought would be to flee. But does one's theology of ministry allow that thought without remainder? How does one discern the issue between releasing one's family and staying to minister? What is it that compels staying in one's place?

Luther can be of help in the discernment process.[10] In 1523 he wrote a fourteen-page letter to John Hess of Breslau, a city under siege by the plague. I will not reconstruct the entire letter but report enough of Luther's counsel to shed some light on the decision making process. He acknowledges the propriety of wanting to preserve one's own life and the propriety of doing so provided some conditions are met. To neglect one in need is to commit murder. Public officials have a duty to remain so that all public services are maintained. As for pastors, they should determine if all pastors in a given place are required to remain. What criteria would be established, especially given American denominationalism, to discern such release from place or such obligation to place? All efforts are to be made to counteract the disease. All forms of healthcare that are required place special obligations on those who can discharge such duties. The fear of death needs to be met head on by the promises of God and the resurrection of Christ. Hence ministers of Word and Sacrament are indispensable.

I must confess I have never asked myself about this issue before the newscasts about the outbreak of bird flu. But is it not part of one's ordinational maturity to ask beforehand just how the ministry of Word and Sacrament both enables and requires fidelity to a place?

10. Luther, *Letters,* 230–44.

The second scenario: Since my retirement from my professorship I have been available for pastoral work at a shelter for victims of domestic abuse and sexual violence. I also completed the sixty-hour course required by the State of Illinois to serve as an advocate for such victims at Freedom House in Princeton, Illinois. I started exactly where Clinton Morrison argued all baptized people begin the Christian life regardless of age: as an infant. This was all new to me. I was an "ordinational infant" here, being taught and tested by those who extended me credit by saying, "I'd like to talk to a pastor." I learned a lot in sixty hours of lectures, videos, and stories, enough hardly.

I now know what Thomas Troeger meant in his novel *A Parable of Ten Preachers*, when he writes about preaching to a congregation where knowingly or unknowingly the preacher does not ask how such victimized persons in the congregation might hear a conventional sermon.[11] One example: A preacher launched into a sermon on justification by grace through faith, waxing eloquent about the gospel. An abused woman found herself increasingly distressed by the question, why does the victimizer always seem to benefit by the justification of sinners (not the sin) while victims bear shame and hurt and hear nothing about justice? Justification by grace through faith always seems to advantage the victimizer. What is gospel to the abused?

Third scenario: Ordinational maturation has come about by officiating at three multiethnic weddings. I knew nothing of the wedding customs of three different Asian peoples until asked to incorporate such customs into the liturgy. None of the customs posed any threat to the integrity of the Christian faith; in fact the customs offered opportunities for the homily to integrate scripture and national cultures. For example, at one, the tea ceremony, served with the most formal protocols of hospitality of welcome to the bride's and groom's families, afforded the opportunity to preach on the "cup"; many cup texts exist in scripture. But I had to be tutored in the basics from three different traditions. Ordinational maturation opened ways of service I never thought of on the day I was ordained! To resist such maturation is to resist ministry.[12]

---

11. Troeger, *Parable*, ch. 2.

12. The book I found to be most helpful is Black, *Worship across Cultures*. In it twenty-one ethnic heritages and/or people groups are introduced together with their unique practices of the Christian rites and sacraments.

The more scope there is to one's ministry the more ignorance will be revealed. But that is all for the good, as St. Paul said, that we might continue "to study to show ourselves approved workers who have no need to be ashamed, rightly diving the word of truth." The people who extend credit to us will not be taking foolish risks and our ministry just may be spared both arrogance and abdication. If so, it will be because we have not ceased in our ordinational maturation.

Yet there is the larger issue of "bearing rule in the church," which also is part of the authorization given in the Evangelical Covenant Church to those ordained to Word and Sacrament. "Bearing rule" and "sharing service" go together. The exercise of authority in leadership shows itself, for example, in pastoral discretion regarding one's officiating at weddings or baptisms. Such matters are decided after prayer and conversation. But "bearing rule" has a public side in governance and leadership.

St. Ignatius of Antioch spoke of the church at Rome as "holding the chief place in love,"[13] or ranking "first in love,"[14] or even "presiding in love,"[15] translations that hold a compelling denominator to say the least for a congregation. To preside over an assembly of love is no small skill. I am drawn to a term used by Pastor Jim Kitchens for what wise pastors (presiders over the assembly of love) might be called as they function as resident theologians in guiding congregations to practice careful, caring, and apt critical conversations over extended time when having to come to terms with a crucial issue: "discernmentarian" (note the analogy with parliamentarian).

Let us say the congregation is conflicted over the war issue: there are some young people who want support for conscientious objector status, and there are also persons who have been wounded and families who have lost someone. A "discernmentarian" helps persons come to terms with their baptismal identity as persons, their eucharistic identity as a congregation, their capabilities as a priesthood of all believers and as citizens of a nation. Adapting Kitchens' description of the process used in his parish, it might look something like this:

13. Srawley, trans., *Epistles of St. Ignatius*, 29.

14. Richardson, ed., *Early Christian Fathers*, 103.

15. For the debate on the possible meanings of this phrase, see Quasten, *Patrology*, 69–70. The Roman Church ranked high in charitable contributions. The term may also imply some form of Roman honor, maybe authority.

1. Biblical Study

    Texts dealing with relations to the state

    Texts of violence

    The Sermon on the Mount

    Texts dealing with enemies

2. Church History and Theology

    The history and doctrine of just war

    The history and doctrine of pacifism

    The state and conscience

3. Testimonials

    From military personnel

    From pacifists and those who did alternate service

4. Work toward Formulating Life Together

My point is that "bearing rule in the church" via the work of the discernmentarian bears greatly on the parliamentarian. The latter presses for a vote, often with haste and without resolving much of anything. A process of discernment is not a quick fix. But in the end the process has had time to work and be worked. The process aims at the sufficient preparation of both *heart* and *mind.* Parliamentary procedure can turn out to be a game of wits that only a few initiates can play. In the process of discernment, the church has become a theological community and has, hopefully, learned to think together with scripture. In the discernment process, which does not replace parliamentary procedure, it is desired that the parliamentary process is more fruitful, less conflicted, and less prone to power maneuvers. And that is where pastoral rule ought to show its colors: returning people to the "third thing," the scriptures. Such a procedure I submit is a safeguard for the congregation against abuse and the pastor against abdication. The procedure is not foolproof but it is faith-based, which, in the Christian community, is a virtue, not a vice as Kitchens says: "Post-moderns . . . have a deep desire to belong to a *community* rather than an *organization.* Developing more communal, less formally bureaucratic polities that allow their voices—and everyone else's—to be heard will help make our congregations the kinds of communities they seek."[16] This stands a good chance of becoming an assembly of charity. Underneath it all, this form of bearing rule is governance as pastoral care.

---

16. Kitchens, *Postmodern Parish*, 85–99. See also the chapter "Moral Deliberations in Congregations" by Brent Coffin in Bave et al., *Taking Faith Seriously*, which details a congregational process used by the Trinity Covenant Church, Lexington, MA, and its "discernmentarian-pastor," Chris Haydon.

4

Word

Vow: Will you be diligent in your reading and study of the Holy Scripture, and seek knowledge of those things that make you a stronger and more able minister of Jesus Christ?

Answer: I will with the help of God.

Vow: Will you undertake to be a faithful pastor, caring for God's people, nourishing them in the preaching and teaching of the word . . . ?

Answer: I will with the help of God.[1]

THE POINT OF THIS chapter is this: those who hold preaching and teaching offices in the church are first hearers of the word, then its proclaimers. It is both insufficient and in the end tragic if the qualifications for pastoral office do not specify hearing along with exegetical, pastoral, and homiletical competencies. When hearing is not included in the mandated specifications for office, the end result becomes tragic because it reinforces the monological, authoritarian, and elitist side of the ministry. An omission of hearing, by design or more likely default, results in the pastor or teacher being the source of his or her own authority. Even more critical, the absence of a disciplined habit of listening to the Word of God in scripture results in the scripture being reduced to a source for sermons, lessons, and theological argument. While the scriptures are at the center of the pastoral vocation, they have not achieved their end by being a means to the "professional" requirement of a weekly sermon or lecture. Let us write it large in our "job description" (pardon my heretical but culturally correct term!): Our first obligation is

1. *The Covenant Book,* 406.

as hearer of the Word just as the vow to be a diligent reader of scripture precedes the vow to preach and teach scripture. The Word is served first and foremost by being heard by those whose office it is to proclaim it.

So how does the preacher hear the word before even preaching the sermon to him/herself? Robert Farrar Capon has his usual frontal way of putting it:

> . . . unless we're willing to be blind to the certainties of religion by which we've lived all our lives, we'll never be able to hear the Word of God, let alone preach it. For the blind depend on hearing to a degree that seeing never comes close to . . . we're called to come to them (the scriptures) blind to every thing religion ever told us we're told to expect, and just *hear them.* Because while seeing may be an analogy to knowledge, *hearing* is the classic analogue of *faith.* And faith is always *trust* in a person's *word.*[2]

Capon is of course picking up on an ancient pattern: reading was done "out loud." Alberto Manguel's *A History of Reading* shows just how decisive this practice was thought to be. The text became a conversation and when a word was sounded it was in effect the voice of the absent partner. Moreover, the word on a page was motionless, the spoken word was mobile. In fact, Manguel reports that the first regulations requiring monks to keep silent in the scriptorium occurs in the ninth century.[3] Capon reports that St. Augustine's first encounter with silent reading was upon seeing it. Ambrose of Milan was so doing.[4]

Another factor at work may need to be acknowledged as pertinent to the preacher's hearing of the word of God. I come by it from poet Beth Ann Fennelly in regard to her discipline of committing one hundred poems to memory. But it is the saying of the lines that generates the surplus of meaning. She testifies:

> I don't begin by thinking: *And now I will commit this poem to memory.*
> Instead, I'm reading a poem. It's a poem I've read before, but suddenly the letters turn into doors that yield to the touch. I have

2. Capon, *Foolishness of Preaching*, 46.

3. Manguel, *History*, 45. See the entire chapter "The Silent Reader." For further elaboration of these themes, see Wiseman, "Books," and Roberts, "Books," both in *The Cambridge History of the Bible* vol. 1.

4. Capon, *Foolishness of Preaching*, 61–63.

the urge to say it aloud. It's delicious on the tongue: *mouth feel* is what the food scientists call this. I repeat it again, and again.[5]

For want of a better term, the culinary metaphor of *mouth feel* holds promise for preachers. Words, like foods, have texture, taste, color, memories, dread, anticipation and the like. They have a foretaste and leave an aftertaste. Foods have to be bitten, chewed, smelled and swallowed to not only get their metabolic value but also to get their "mouth feel," a kind of aesthetic term that may suggest even a period of time to get adjusted.

Reading out loud is the equivalent to biting, chewing, smelling, and swallowing, especially when the reading is not speed-reading or goal oriented. Words need to be heard. That is where the "digestive" process starts, where faith is born or awakened. The reader is the other partner to the conversation. Rereading aloud can be like asking for repetition, like taking a second bite of something one did not like the taste of the first time. My mother's repeated counsel to me was, "Take another bite," like with asparagus, which I did not like. Afterwards she would say, "See, it wasn't so bad." Like Capon's metaphor, seeing and tasting the Word opened blind eyes. Is it possible that the "mouth feel," the matter of "taste," while liable to being subjective in the worst way do in their own ways allude to a necessary reality, namely discernment. Both "mouth feel" and "taste" are terms that point to something, like a person's palate learning to know its way around food.

So the reader, especially the one who reads "out loud," develops, in the act of pronunciation, a "mouth feel" for words, a hearing palate if you will, for the texture and trajectory of a word or sentence. Such subtleties escape seeing. The ears become orifices of nourishment, or in some cases, worse. Hearers first. The other partner waits to be heard. Take up and hear.

Two biblical texts are crucial to the point of this chapter. The first one is Hebrews 4:12–13: "Indeed the word of God is living and active, sharper than any two—edged sword, piercing until it divides soul from spirit, joint from narrow; it is able to judge the thoughts and intentions of the heart. And before him no creature is hidden, but all are naked and laid bare to the eyes of the one to whom we must render account." As for this text, *the scripture reads us*! Even though we perform the act

5. Fennelly, "My Hundred," 35.

of reading, the action is in the passive voice: the reader is being diagrammed in a way no less rigorous than if the reader were diagramming a sentence determining the nouns, verbs, adjectives, and adverbs and how they function as the subject, verb, modifiers, and object in the sentence.

Frederick Buechner's pointed words have a transparency consistent in every way with the intent of this text:

> A particular truth can be stated in words—that life is better than death and love than hate, that there is a god or is not, that light travels faster than sound and cancer can sometimes be cured if you discover it in time. But truth itself is another matter, the truth that Pilate asked for, tired and bored and depressed by his long day. Truth itself cannot be stated. Truth simply is, and is what is, the good with the bad, the joy with the despair, the presence and absence of God, the swollen eye, the bird pecking the cobbles for crumbs. Before it is a word, the gospel that is truth is silence, a pregnant silence in its ninth month, and in answer to Pilate's question, Jesus keeps silent, even with his hands tied behind him manages somehow to hold silence out like a terrible gift.[6]

And:

> What Jesus hits Pilate over the head with is Pilates himself. Jesus just stands there in silence in a way that throws Pilate back on his own silence, the truth of himself.[7]

How clever then that Jesus chose to "hit people over the head" with themselves or to throw them back on their own silence by preaching in parables! Parables mirrored people back to themselves. Listeners could "see themselves" in what they heard. I once heard an African-American preacher say that good preaching puts the eyes in people's ears! The parables do that, to the point of painful clarity and without need to add a moral. The word will do its own work. Read Nathan's parabolic rebuke of David after his affair with Bathsheba and murder of Uriah (1 Kgs 12) or Daniel's interpretations of the king's dreams (Dan 2, 4, 5). Examples of the work of Jesus might include Luke 7:36–50; 10:25–37; and 16:19–31.

Walter Brueggemann argues that the virtue of this poetic style is that it capacitates hearers for three responses:

6. Buechner, *Telling the Truth*, 16.
7. Ibid., 17.

1. to wonder beyond certitude;

2. to ask beyond one's answers;

3. to seek beyond one's rationality.[8]

The reason Brueggemann finds the manner of the gospel resistant exclusively to prose and to frontal confrontation is that it may only reinforce a sense of autonomy in the hearer, generating perhaps resistance in the form of argumentation and defensiveness. The poetic, parabolic approach, on the other hand, comes upon one in ways that maintain an element of surprise and subvert domesticated expectations.[9] In this fashion the hearer, and I may add reader, is drawn into a vortex or power field of energies that brings one face to face with One who is calling out to the reader/hearer of the words and voice.

When we allow ourselves sustained hearing of the word perhaps two words are needed to explicate the paradoxical outcome:

The reader is both judged and justified by the same Justice.

The reader is both exposed and covered by the same Revealer.

How to live in the middle of this paradox is the real Kierkegaardian feat! But Hebrews does not leave us without recourse. "For we do not have a high priest who is unable to sympathize with us in our weaknesses, but we have one who in every respect has been tested as we are, yet without sin. Let us therefore approach the throne of grace with boldness, so that we may receive mercy and find grace to help in time of need" (4:15–16). Furthermore we are encouraged by the same author to "have confidence to enter the sanctuary by the blood of Jesus . . . [therefore] let us approach with a true heart in full assurance of faith, with our hearts sprinkled clean from an evil conscience and our bodies washed with pure water" (10:19–22).

Similar texts can be drawn upon where simultaneously one is both exposed and covered, invited and intimidated, accused and atoned for. For example, after the resurrection Jesus asks Peter three times if he loves him. St. Augustine said the threefold inquiry was necessary for Peter to face, work through, and be released from his threefold denial of Jesus.[10] Both forces are at work: judgment and justification, exposure and covering, examples all of law and gospel. In Revelation 1:17ff, the

8. Brueggemann, *Finally Comes*, 137 (see also 77).

9. Ibid., 13.

10. Augustine, *Sermon 295*, 1653–54.

apostle John envisions himself prostrate in front of the Son of Man re-splendent as he is in purity and glory only to hear the words, "Get up." This paradoxical confrontation, said the Pietist exegete Johann Albrecht Bengel, both frightened and fortified John.[11] Perhaps that same sort of fright and fortification is what is described in Isaiah 6. Are not these examples of Brueggemann's less than prose and frontal attack and more a word that capacitates people to wonder beyond their certitude, ask beyond their answers, and seek beyond their rationality? Or Buechner's equivalent of the indirect if not totally silent Jesus letting "Peter get hit over the head with Peter and John with John"?

My contention is that only in the posture of sustained hearing will we receive the confidence to abide the presence of the Holy One whom we serve when we know and come to know that which breeds a sense of disqualification. We can forego the hearing and surge forward in our work, ignoring the warning signs of spiritual fatigue and hypocrisy, or we can diligently hear the word so that the work of Malachi's refiner's fire equips us to stand before God and others, confident by grace to speak with conviction but not contempt (Mal 3:2).

The existential condition of those in pastoral office is that often they are strung out between

> Willpower and weariness
> Determination and discouragement
> Resolve and reluctance
> Sensing invitation and intimidation by the Holy One
> With faith yet fearful
> Life more exacting than exciting
> Life more testy than triumphant.

I have told my students in spiritual formation that one cannot learn anything about oneself that is not already atoned for. Each time a new facet, memory, fact or issue from one's life comes to light, it is not like the Christian life begins all over. The suffering of one atonement is meant to give the security and confidence to name it and release it in the name of God. The Holy Spirit reveals such matters incrementally because absolute self-knowledge all at once would kill one. Scripture continues to "read" us so that we may grow in the confidence rooted in grace to be truthful and so enjoy the freedom of the gospel.

---

11. Bengelii, *Sechzig Erbaulicher*, 48, 63.

The second way to read scripture is in 2 Timothy 2:15: "Do your best to present yourself to God as one approved by him, a worker who has no need to be ashamed, rightly explaining the word of truth." This pertains to what we are trained to do: exegete scripture, using the best skills and tools our training has provided; utilize the auxiliary courses—church history and theology—to provide interpretation that accords with wisdom and has a tested quality; exegete culture via the best methods pastoral theology has taught us. In this case, the *reverse* of what was said of Hebrews 4 obtains: it is we who now read scripture subjecting it to the most rigorous questions and use of tools at our disposal. As St. Paul said, we are rightly to explain the word of truth so that we will have no need for shame.

I am not of the impression that St. Paul thinks such a person will have spoken with such competence and spirituality that it will be as if the last word has been uttered. This is not about having the last word: Rightly explaining the word of truth is a test of those in pastoral office to embrace the intellectual demands of their office and to acknowledge that pastoral identity cannot honorably and honestly be embraced apart from serving as the resident theologian in the congregation served. No one is helped, least of all him or her in pastoral office, by saying, "Well, you know, I'm only a pastor, not a theologian." If those in local pastoral office are not theologians, who are?

By default the members of the congregation will look elsewhere for intellectual leadership. Or even worse, the congregation will gradually draw the conclusion that church is not the place to do critical and creative thinking, to deal systematically and historically with issues that call for the mind to do its God-given work: think. Church is the place for questions and it needs to be safe to ask them—safe from ridicule, dismissal, and quick answers.

Scientific issues loom large today. I saw a church billboard that purported to deal with a scientific issue. Line 1: The Big Bang. Line 2: You've Got to Be Kidding: God. Can one imagine a young person working in college in the field of cosmology coming home to that and hoping to get an honest hearing to questions?

Think of the complexity of rightly dividing the issue between just war theory and pacifism. The issue belongs in church because 1) church history shows the persistent polarization both in and among churches even up to now, and 2) the presence of these positions in local congregations. Pastorally I have been asked to support the CO status for a person of draft age (Viet Nam era). My point is that the resident theologian should be able to offer a congregation a reasonable introduction as to 1) how both sides read the Bible and especially the crucial texts, 2) how various Christian thinkers have developed each viewpoint so that parishioners know the main points and structure of each argument, and 3) how to relate to one another when, in a time of national military involvement, congregants differ so that people will not end up accusing each other of lack of patriotism or lack of biblical integrity.

As I have set out the resident theologian's task, the task is not to solve this issue. The task is to help congregants make a theologically and biblically informed judgment and to set forth an ecclesiology that fosters teachableness among all. But to do this well two issues need to be set forth:

1. Interpretation is a moral act. Pastoral interpretation means that one knows the view opposite one's own or even a view that needs to be opposed well enough to present it on it's own terms. "Rightly explaining the word of truth" includes the morality of explanation and truthful presentation of material.

2. That we are committed to the intellectual work of the ministry, that ideas matter and that it is a pastoral responsibility to have a disciplined curriculum of study.

Vocationally speaking, "rightly explaining the word of truth" becomes most visible in preaching and teaching. In some ways this is the most public face of the ministry and for that reason can be unduly tempting and unmitigatingly discouraging. Tempting: it's a place to "have the limelight." Discouraging: it's a place where expectations are sometimes never realized.

As for the tempting part, let me begin with Reinhold Niebuhr. In *Leaves from the Notebook of a Tamed Cynic*, written in the midst of his pastoral work in Detroit, Niebuhr, writing of the intellectual work of study, says that the purpose of such is "to reveal the relativity of all things so that pulpit utterances do not become too extravagant, and let the pulpit save the student from sinking in a sea of relativities." Every truth, he argues, no matter how qualified, has a portion that is essentially absolute and therefore worth proclaiming. Further, in agreement he cites a Greek author that "all oratory is based on half truths." Then he confesses,

> I notice that the tendency of extravagance in the pulpit and on the platform increases with the size of the crowd. As my congregation increases in size I become more unguarded in my statements. Wherefore may the good Lord deliver me from being a popular preacher.[12]

John Updike's novel *In the Beauty of the Lillies* chronicles the gradual distancing of the Rev. Clarence Wilmot from his calling as a Presbyterian pastor to his final compulsion to leave pastoral ministry altogether. He has a daughter, Esther, now Alma DeMott, who is an actress, even to the extent of sharing the stage with Bing Crosby. She noticed, as Crosby aged, a certain flash of impatience and coldness. Updike's description of Alma's assessment of Crosby and herself is a cautionary tale even for clergy:

> A certain inhuman efficiency had to lie at the heart of such achievement. She observed in him what she already sensed in herself, the danger of becoming a performer purely, of coming alive in proportion to the size of the audience and being absent minded and remote when the audience was small.[13]

Someone has said that to be a good preacher one has to be a good actor but woe to the preacher who is an actor. Apparently poets know of a conflict between two poets within themselves. So Ted Kooser, a poet laureate of the United States:

> I was an artificial poet. The two sides of being a poet—the poet as celebrity and the poet as writer.
> Yet there are still two poets present—the one who quietly concentrates on perfecting the poem and the one who wants to be celebrated and adored. I'm delighted and nourished by the first poet and embarrassed by the second.[14]

Preachers and teachers: the one thing that separates us from being actors, being satisfied with artificiality and from seeking celebrity status, is "being read" by Hebrews 4:12–13, where this chapter started. When we let ourselves hear this word, when we know every part of us is being

---

12. Niebuhr, *Leaves*, 56–57.
13. Updike, *In the Beauty*, 353.
14. Kooser, *Poetry Home Repair*, 4–5.

read like an open book, just maybe it is safe to enter the pulpit or get behind the lectern.

This public act of pulpit or lectern requires a maturing spiritual discernment to prevent, on the one hand, a contentment with artificiality, which to a certain extent sells, and on the other hand, a covetousness for celebrity status which acquires market value. On the other hand, the occupant of the pulpit or lectern can easily succumb to discouragement in a culture that thrives on instant gratification and measures most "successes" in quantitative terms. In terms of St. Paul's assessment, some plant seeds of the gospel, some water the seeds, but God gives the growth. As if to inculcate a deeper humility, St. Paul says that neither the planter nor the waterer are anything but only God, since the one who plants and the one who waters have one purpose, and that is to work together on God's building or in God's field. In any case, all one is doing is building on another's work (1 Cor 3:6–10).

At the end of Hebrews 11, the chapter recalling what God accomplished through the faith of so many persons, even some of the "lesser ones," the writer of Hebrews tells his readers that all of those sampled in the list will be made perfect through them (11:40). And so it is: we of the year 2009, 2010, 2011, ___, ___ are the perfection of the generations of saints and apostles who preceded us. It is not a popular thought that we *perfect* our antecedents; it seems nearly incomprehensible. But the gift hidden in the statement is that all servants of the gospel, no matter how faithful, *will not finish*. This is a gift because it can preserve us from developing a messianic complex. The grace hidden in the statement is that each and all servants of the gospel can live a fulfilled life despite the unfinished task. Someone will perfect us just as Hebrews 11:40 says the readers of that text perfected Abraham, Moses, Rahab, etc. We entered into someone else's labor when we entered the ministry; someone will take up where we leave off. This is meant for our contentment: some plant and some water while God gives the increase, but neither the planter nor the waterer have the competitive advantage.

A subsequent observation follows. Servants of the word have an eschatologically oriented vocation. Plainly put, none knows if he or she will harvest their planting and watering. What one knows is that there will be a harvest and that what was begun and/or continued by us will be perfected by another—but perfected it will be. That is the eschatological dimension made plain by Isaiah 55:10–11: "For as the rain and snow came down from heaven and do not return there until they have watered the earth, making it bring forth and sprout, giving seed to the sower and bread to the eater, so shall the word be that goes forth from my mouth: it shall not return to me empty, but it shall accomplish that which I purpose and succeed in the thing for which I sent it." Or that promise to Jeremiah: ". . . I am watching over my word to perform it" (Jer 1:12). Or Jesus' words, "Heaven and earth will pass away, but my words will not pass away" (Matt 24:35).

Theologically speaking, the narrative coherence bears witness that the one and same God who brought Israel out of Egypt and Jesus out of the tomb will, in like manner be faithful to his own word. The preacher and teacher of the gospel will be vindicated although they may not live to see it. But they live by and through this story of God, who does not let his word go to waste and the effort of God's proclaimers is not wasted.

A story might be useful. Loosestrife—*lythrum salicaria*—is either a curse or blessing, a weed or flower, depending on a number of personal proclivities. It can grow up to 10 feet tall, take over a territory around a pond in a hurry, and produce up to 2.7 million seeds per plant! The seeds can lie buried for years and then spring forth when brought to the surface by a disturbance. Writers in this field of botany refer to this as "recruitment from the seed bank."[15]

Seeds—buried, dormant, not dead, kicked into action by a disturbance. Take heart fellow workers: Jesus stressed the soils—deep and fertile, shallow and rocky and hard. Pastoral work is soil work, preparation of the seed bank. Then we wait for the disturbance—a crisis, a visitation of the Holy Spirit to recruit the seed, surface it, and let it sprout.

Back to where we started: can we become hearers of the word that sets us free from anxiety about the word?

This from Emily Dickinson:

> A word is dead
> When it is said
> Some say.
> I say it just
> Begins to live
> That day.[16]

In the meantime,

15. Gutin, "Purple Passion," 76–78.
16. Dickinson, in *Three Centuries*, 395.

> What is it for which the child waits
> at the fold of these dry hills, crouched
> beside a river of sand that holds
> the pattern of flowing water?
>
> Nothing is alive here but our seeds
> rattled from their cases by the wind,
> thirsty for a second coming of rain.[17]

So we are assured of the wind and rain.

---

17. Housley, "Lessons."

5

Water

PASTORS BAPTIZE. THEY ARE authorized to do so by the church in the rite of ordination and, where the rules so authorize, by licensure. Baptism is a public act, an official act adhering to what pastors are called to do. Like preaching, it can easily devolve into "professional service," one more item to be scheduled. But then the pastoral is lost in the professional.

My point in this chapter will be that the officiant at the sacrament of Holy Baptism is first a baptized one, then a baptizer. To approach the font or pool one does not appear in the arrogance of the right to be there. One is there by delegation, not just by the authority of the ordaining body recognized by that local church but by the authority of the One, himself a Baptized One, who told us to use water in his name, the name of the God who sent him and in the name of the Spirit who hovered over the first waters of creation, over the waters of Mary's womb and over the waters of the Jordan at his own baptism.

The baptizer should have this question asked of Jesus' disciples inscribed in his or her pastor's copy of their book of liturgical and pastoral rites, at the beginning of the service of baptism: "Are you able to drink the cup that I drink, or be baptized with the baptism with which I am baptized?" The reply of the disciples ought to give one pause: "We are able." Then Jesus assured them that indeed they would be baptized with the same baptism. (Mark 10:38–39). What the disciples had not counted on was the highly unpredictable issue of their baptismal maturational level once it was their turn to take up their apostolic ministry. Of course they had a foretaste soon after Jesus had spoken these words to them: one denied him; one sold him; the others left him.

When pastors act as baptizer they cannot escape their baptismal identity. God's voice claimed them as beloved as it had done for Jesus. Moreover, the Voice identified with them even as it identified them as ones called to a special service to Word and Sacrament. When one's hands, or feet as in the case of immersion, first touch the water, can one do anything but renew one's own baptism, allowing the magnitude of one's own encounter with the water to do whatever work it needs to do? It is a truism that water seems to be able to find any perforation, hole, or crack in any wall. Water has sovereignty, whether as current or seepage, to find a way in. Water works its way. So can baptism. We are not safe from the waters! Thank God!

One way for the pastor-officiant to appropriate more fully the promise and call embodied in his or her own baptism would be to develop the practice of exploring the multiple word pictures for baptism in the New Testament. Whether one does it on the anniversary of one's baptism or in conjunction with administering the sacrament, these word pictures, either on their own or "totaled up," will present one with an artesian well springing forth life-giving water. Here is my list of such images.

Washing/Cleansing	Acts 22:15–16; 1 Corinthians 6:11; Ephesians 5:26
Rebirth	Titus 3:5
Deliverance from Evil Powers Safety in the Ark	1 Peter 3:18–22
Dying/Rising	Romans 6:1–11; Colossians 2:12
Sign of New Ownership Into the Name; Reception of an Ascribed Identity	Acts 10:48; 1 Corinthians 1:13
Enlightenment/Illumination	Hebrews 6:4–5; 10:33ff
Putting on a Garment	Galatians 3:27
Incorporation into the Body	1 Corinthians 12:13, 26–27
Circumcision	Colossians 2
Seal	2 Corinthians 1:22; Ephesians 1:13–14

Baptized into Moses, in the Cloud, in the Sea: Exodus – Wilderness	1 Corinthians 10:1–5
Identified by Name and Investiture for Service	Baptismal narratives of Jesus

Now, briefly, some commentary. Two Old Testament stories and characters are listed: Moses and the exodus, and Noah and the flood. In both cases there is not only exodus but entrance: out of Egypt (Red Sea), long years in the desert and entrance via waters (Jordan) to the promised land; out of the destructive waters and into the ark; forty days of "ark life"; out of the ark and onto the new creation (recall the use of St. Peter Chrysologus's image that the inhabitants of the ark were "the seedlings of a new creation"). Notice the triadic stages for Moses and Noah: a deliverance, a life in between (desert or ark), and entrance into new life. How would you find yourself in these stories? How in particular do these stories/characters deepen your appropriation of the intent and extent of your baptism?

The Name. I think the image holds a great potential for meditation. One is not baptized into one's own name. Unlike the scene in the film *The Apostle*, we do not baptize ourselves into the Name nor claim, upon such a self-referencing act, that now one speaks for the Name. Instead my attention is drawn to Louis Marie Chauvet as he speaks of a "Third Party witness to baptism": "The new relation with God brought about by baptism is in practice inseparable from a new covenantal relation among the people. The absent-present Other, the Third Party witness in whose name the group is created as the communal 'We' of this new covenant which is the church, has for its name Jesus Christ."[1] Think of a meditation on this event carried out in the name of the present-absent Third Party and of the ascribed identity one has as the Name-bearer. Some themes come to mind. Baptism is never a private act just as one's life is never private. There is no such a thing as a private sin; never can a baptized person live with any adapted version of "what happens in Las Vegas stays in Las Vegas"; it does not and will not. The presence of the "absent Third Party" adds depth to the warning not to take the name of the Lord in vain since by baptism the "Third Party" has given us his name. Finally, it means one has a sponsor, a witness.

1. Chauvet, *Symbol and Sacrament*, 439.

A final example I will offer is based on Galatians 3:27, where we are informed that as many as have been baptized into Christ have put on Christ. When I was first studying Greek I read E. D. Burton's commentary on Galatians and learned that the grammatical construction, with a personal object, means "to put on," in this text meant "to become as" or to "take on the character of."[2] Imagine that, can you? Take on the character of Christ, to put that on as one puts on clothes (see Rom 13:14 and Col 3:9–10). We put on Christ. Really!? I once wrote a meditation for publication on this text saying this is like parents buying clothes many sizes too large for an infant hoping to save some money by letting the infant grow into the clothes. A marriage is something one grows into being way too large for the couple at the time of the ceremony. Persons mature into their professions. Whether marriages or professions, the fullness of either is always future, waiting to fill out. Do we not grow up into Christ?[3] Can you cope with the fact you have put on Christ, that you are with him as a joint heir of God? Daniel W. Hardy and David Ford say that "Coping with God and his generosity is the central task of the Christian faith and what is given stretches all capacity."[4] To do so is at the heart of one's baptismal maturity. But one never outgrows one's baptism. The clothing is always too large.

Perhaps you see my intention. Each reader can appropriate these images in ways that, when one touches the water it comes home to one that one has been washed, birthed, delivered from the powers, died and risen with Christ, is under new ownership, has a "Third Party" witness and sponsor-advocate, has a name to honor in thought, word and deed, that one is thrust by the water into "ark life" (incorporated into the Body of Christ), and eyes opened, illumined to all that has been given in and by the water when, as Luther would unequivocally say, the water is comprehended by the Word of God.[5] Without the word, it is no baptism, only water, bereft of a *command* to do it (I mean, who would dare to claim all these images for him or herself except by divine permission) and bereft of *promise* (that indeed the baptized is God's beloved and chosen), the same word that accompanied the water applied to God's

---

2. Burton, *Galatians*, 203–6.

3. Weborg, "Cling to the Water," 2–3.

4. Hardy and Ford, *Praising*, 71.

5. Small Catechism, questions 1 and 3.

son Jesus. Most often, those clothes do not seem a perfect fit. But the fit is not ours to decide.

At the point of sensing the misfit of the clothing, of bearing the Name or of the spiritual distress generated by those with whom we share space in the ark, two invitations, both destructive, come to our door:

1. To minimize sin and maximize grace

2. To minimize grace and maximize sin

Number one falls victim to the practice of self-justification and presumptive spiritual prowess. Number two falls victim to the practice of distrust of God's mercy in Christ and despair. Number one embodies pride, number two, sloth. It is not our place to minimize or maximize any aspect of our relation to God. It is our place to let be what God has made known to us in Christ and illumined by the Holy Spirit and to let ourselves be without engaging in a form of spiritual self-mutilation. Let these images illumine your eyes of beholding and ears of hearing what has been said and shown.

Both sin and grace have a way of topping emotions, the former in regret and guilt, the latter in release and gratitude. Regret and guilt, release and gratitude have a way of releasing tears. Tears have found their way into the devotional literature in relation to baptism. This from patristic writer John Climacus, "The Fathers have declared the singing of psalms to be a weapon, prayer to be a wall, honest tears to be a bath."[6] More specifically,

> The tears that come after baptism are greater than baptism itself, though it may seem rash to say so. Baptism washes off those evils that were previously within us, whereas the sins committed after baptism are washed away by tears. The baptism received by us as children we have all defiled, but we cleanse it anew with our tears. If God in His love for the human race had not given us tears, those being saved would be few indeed and hard to find.[7]

Tears are like a second baptism. This poetic text from George Herbert, writing out of a seventeenth-century time of ministry in England conflicted three ways by religious controversy, an ample environment for pastoral despair and resentment, sets out a telling baptismal recollection:

6. Climacus, *Ladder*, 93. Climacus lived c. 579–649.

7. Ibid., 137.

HOLY BAPTISM

As He that sees a dark and shady grove,
    Stays not, but looks beyond it on the sky;
    So when I view my sins, mine eyes remove
More backward still, and to that water fly,
      Which is above the heav'ns, whose spring and rent
        Is in my dear Redeemer's pierced side,
        O blessed streams! either ye to prevent
      And stop our sins from growing thick and wide.
Or else give tears to drown them, as they grow.
    In you Redemption measures all my time,
    And spreads the plaister equal to the crime:
You taught the Book of Life my Name, that so
    Whatever future sins should me miscall,
    Your first acquaintance might discredit all.[8]

By calling and authorization the baptized becomes a baptizer. In so doing he or she is carrying out a divine commandment, Matthew 28:18–20, and carrying on a story. The command is story, having its virtue in the lengthy narrative of God's watery ways of doing God's work. The quotation below is a portion of the baptismal liturgy of the Evangelical Covenant Church. Note how it conforms to the "narrative coherence" described in chapter 1. The narrative recalls the decisive role water played in the history of salvation. The prayer, which invokes the Holy Spirit, does so indicating both narrative and images from the history of salvation and asks that this baptism about to be administered become a part of that narrative. Where Jesus' command to baptize is carried out a story is carried on and the same Spirit present at creation and at Jesus' baptism is now called down on this baptism of this/these people in this place. So,

We give you particular thanks, O God,
as we recall your redemption by water:
over it your Spirit hovered at creation;
your righteous servant Noah and his family survived in the ark;
through it your people passed in deliverance from slavery;
you gave them water from the rock in the desert;
through it your people walked again to the promise land;
in it the foreigner Namaan was cleansed of leprosy;
by it Jesus was safeguarded in Mary's womb;
in it your Son Jesus was baptized,

8. Herbert, *Country Parson*, 157–58.

and by it, declared solidarity with sinners;
at his crucifixion blood and water came forth in sacrifice for
humankind;
at his resurrection he was made alive for our justification.

Just prior to his ascension he commanded us, saying:

"All authority in heaven and on earth has been given to me.
Go therefore and make disciples of all nations,
baptizing them in the name of the Father and of the Son
and of the Holy Spirit,
and teaching them to obey everything that I have commanded you.
And remember, I am with you always, to the end of the age."
Water of life, Jesus our light; journey from death to new life.
Water of life, Jesus our light; journey from death to new life.
Let us pray.
O God, let your Spirit hover over this water as at creation
and as this same Spirit came over Jesus Christ at his baptism,
so let the Spirit come now, making this:
> *a washing with water by the word;*
> *a sign of the new covenant;*
> *our habitat in Christ, crucified and risen;*
> *our bonding in water with brothers and sisters in Christ;*
> *our solidarity with those with whom he is in solidarity;*
> *and our commissioning to serve in Jesus' name. Amen.*[9]

Chapter 1 quoted William Manson as referring to the "time structure" of the biblical narrative as "a structure of Divine acts in which all
the parts are held together." So a pastor administering baptism is a part
of the "time structure," a continuation of Divine activity in continuity
with the previous divine acts. Hence the narrative coherence of the
Covenant Church's baptismal liturgy printed above.[10]

While this chapter has no intention of setting out a complete
theology of baptism, these are select themes that relate to the spiritual
health of the baptizer. First, one is *incorporated* into Christ, having put
on Christ, misfit though it seems, unfit though it feels, no matter: God
(the Voice) *ascribes identity*: My Beloved, My Chosen. Having identified with us Jesus is in position to *identify* us to God. Then God gives
us the Holy Spirit to work at an interior convincement when reasons

9. *The Covenant Hymnal*, no. 934.

10. See:Weborg, "Say and Do Baptism," 267–80, for an analysis of nine denominational baptismal liturgies.

enough accumulate to sabotage this new found confidence: ". . . it is that very Spirit bearing witness with our spirit that we are children of God, and if children, then heirs of God and joint heirs with Christ . . ." (Rom 8:16–17).

Second, *incorporation* into Christ coincides with *initiation* unto a community. The text in Galatians 3:27–28 that informs the baptized that he or she has put on Christ also informs such that the clothing put on can include Jew and Greek, slave or free, male and female—all in one place that can be described, as was mentioned previously as "ark life." Pastor Linnea Carnes, now serving Immanuel Evangelical Covenant Church in Chicago, reports fourteen nationalities and people groups in the congregation.[11] Ark life! Seedlings of the new creation! Galatians 3:27–28 joins 1 Corinthians 12:13 in being the most radical texts on baptismal sociology. The act of baptism cannot be abstracted from the sociology God sets in motion by means of its administration. The "Third Party witness" attests to the event to which other baptized members of the congregation are party. When such persons as present at Immanuel are discriminated against, the "Name" of the "Third Party witness" is taken in vain since the Witness has given us his name as an *ascribed identity*: followers of Jesus Christ, Christian.

Third, once *incorporated* into Christ and *initiated* into the community, the newly baptized are *invested* with the Holy Spirit (which fell on Jesus at his baptism equipping him for his ministry) and *installed* in their respective ministries (the same Spirit continues to equip and call persons, 1 Cor 12:4ff; Eph 4:11ff). Protestants have especially treasured the term, "priesthood of all believers." Speaking specifically of the Evangelical Covenant Church, with origins in Lutheran soil, we find ourselves instructed by Luther who teaches that all of the "baptized are equally priests . . . ,"[12] a teaching restated by Spener in his catechism

---

11. Fredrickson, "Cultural Change," 4.

    Two works will greatly enhance one's understanding of the initiation-incorporation theme as it concerns an increasingly diverse Body of Christ: Conde-Frazier et al., *Many Colored Kingdom*; and Griffin and Walker, *Living on the Borders*.

12. Luther, *To the Christian Nobility*, 129–32.

    Readers should be mindful of Timothy J. Wengert's *Priesthood, Pastors, Bishops; Public Ministry for the Reformation and Today* for a cogently argued critique of the *popular* notion of the priesthood of believers as it has developed in Lutheranism, enabled, in Wengert's view, by Pietism. What he critiques vigorously is any notion of the priesthood of believers as constituting the laity as a distinct entity from the clergy. Instead Wengert argues for the priesthood of all, made so in baptism, and the pastoral

on "The Spiritual Priesthood,"[13] thus bequeathing to the Pietism that shaped the Covenant Church a rich use of 1 Peter 2:9: "But you are a chosen race, a royal priesthood, a holy nation, God's own people in order that you might proclaim the mighty acts of him who called you out of darkness into his marvelous light," all in narrative coherence with, and the continuing development of, the "time structure" of Exodus 19:6. But St. Peter, using Hosea 1:9 and 2:23, specifies the ascribed identity those exiles and aliens, Christians all, scattered in a few geographical areas have in common: once they were no people, now they are God's people and this people is both royal and priestly! Having much suffering and displacement in common, they are to be like new born infants so that they may grow into salvation, that is baptismal maturity. This text, using Old Testament antecedents, is as concerned with a baptismal sociology as Galatians 3:27–28 and 1 Corinthians 12:12–13 but with an added dimension: the congregations receiving this letter, comprised with as diverse people as Immanuel Congregation in Chicago, are to bear in mind that it is their very sociology, their make up and public character, that are their primary proclamation of the gospel. This is life in the ark! Seedlings of a new creation!

One thing remains. Each congregant is by virtue of their baptism and investiture of the Holy Spirit, endowed with gifts and graces to carry out a calling in the world. Among the baptized people of God, there emerges a distinction. Luther taught our ancestors that although "we are all equally priests, we cannot all publicly minister and teach."[14] More recently Leonard Sweet speaks of the basic distinction among the people of God as between baptized ministers (everyone) and ordained ministers (those who make the ministry of the former possible by equip-

---

office by some for the sake of the gospel. But in no sense does the authority for this office derive from the already existing priesthood. God is the authorizing agent via the external means of Word and Sacrament, which creates both the congregation and the office of the ministry as the agency of proclamation but *all* remain part of the priesthood of believers.

   Emmet E. Eklund's *Peter Fjellstedt: Missionary Mentor to Three Continents* shows that some movements within Swedish Pietism did not succumb to the substance of Wengert's critique. Fjellstedt, who influenced both Augustana and to some extent the Mission Friends (later the Covenant Church), was influenced by the German Pietist Johann Albrect Bengel, and neither thought the pastoral office had its source in the priesthood of believers.

   13. Spener, " Spiritual Priesthood," 51.

   14. Luther, *To the Christian Nobility,* 129–32.

ping and training them for ministry) and not between clergy and laity.[15] Taking Ephesians 4 at face value, namely that pastors equip the saints for the work of the ministry, which Sweet's proposal does, I have formulated my own working description of pastoral theology: the art and science of the development of the priesthood of the congregation.

Recently two exegetes have made reference to a particular use of the Greek word for freedom (*eleutheria*), although it must be recognized that this use has a *deeply painful source*: the work done by servants and/or slaves meant freedom for the one freed by their labor.[16] If one may, while acknowledging this exploitative origin, apply this in the pastoral context, might it not mean that pastors could know a freedom in ministry in deeply resourceful ways if they were freed to do their specialized work of equipping and thus "sending" the baptized into their appropriate ministries? (I have appended an outline of my attempts at this during one of my pastorates in Addendum 2).

a. The deployment of increasing numbers of the baptized in ministry multiplies the ministry of all.

b. The amount of "wasted" and unused gifts and skills is increasingly reduced, increasing a sense of satisfaction among congregants.

c. More persons and situations can be cared for.

d. Pastoral work can recover a sense of Sabbath, in that stress over "too much to do, too little time," together with defeatism and guilt, stand a good chance of amelioration unless one is so addicted to control that one cannot release the ministry to the Holy Spirit who has given these persons as gifts of freedom to the pastor.

Incorporated into Christ and ascribed the identity of his name, initiated into the Body of Christ and its place in the larger narrative of the Triune God's work in the redemption of creation, baptized and baptizer are installed and invested with the gifts and graces for their place of service in the Divine project of redemption.

Below I have appended a homily to be included in a service of the reaffirmation of one's baptism. There is a reference to oil, which indicates that such a service may include anointing either in a service of healing or in special prayers for the freedom of the Holy Spirit to be at work.

15. Leonard Sweet, *Faith Quakes*, 142–45, cited in: Frambach, "Models of Leadership," 382. See Addendum 1.

16. Cf. Grieb, " One Who Called You"; and Fredrickson, "No Noose Is Good News."

RENEWAL OF BAPTISM AND ANOINTING

The rooster is among the first evangelists.[17] Hippolytus tells us that at the crowning of the rooster let them pray over the water. Let the water be pure and flowing. The first crowing of the rooster is the time for baptism. Dawn. But we know another crowing of the rooster—the time Peter denied and cursed Jesus.[18] Maybe at the same time. Dawn.

Paradox: the time of the deepest desertion is the same time as that of deepest devotion. Dawn: the border between darkness and light. Baptism: the border between death and birth.[19] When we hear the rooster we hear our end and our beginning.

We have opportunity to renew our baptism and to be renewed by the same Holy Spirit who descended on Jesus at his baptism. The Spirit outfitted him for survival in the wilderness, for resistance to every distraction, with the graces of character and gifts of service needed for doing the will of God.

Isaiah promised that when we passed through the water God would be with us, that the river would not overwhelm us, and even a walk through fire would leave us unblistered.[20]

Our experience may threaten our confidence in these promises. Burned out in service of the gospel—overwhelmed by needs beyond our competence or our consecration. No end in sight either to the fire or to the water.

The crowing of the rooster may make us more mindful of denial than devotion, of the betrayer than the baptized. St. Peter was both! An so there is an invitation to come to the water and to the oil so that the fragrance we smell—pleasing to our nostrils—is the fragrance we are in Christ and to others.[21] In this case oil and water mix, blending into the gifts and graces needed for ministry.

17. Hippolytus, *Apostolic Tradition*, 21, 45.

18. Luke 22:54–62.

19. Cyril, *Lectures*, 61. Which says, "Water of salvation was at once your grave and your mother."

20. Isai 43:1–21.

21. 1 Cor 2:15–16.

6

Bread and Wine

THE CELEBRANT OF HOLY Communion is a communicant before he/
she is a celebrant. Those of us in vocational ministry have a place
at the table before being entrusted with a position at the table. Knowing
how to be at that place is part of one's baptismal maturation, there by
invitation only, not by right and celebrant by installation only, not by
entitlement. Baptismal maturation discerns whether or not one's spiritual pattern is to maximize one's sins and deficiencies so as to minimize
the freedom of grace or to maximize the freedom of grace so as to be
irresponsible about one's habits, sense of self, pretense such as to claim
a righteousness and spiritual health that is not present. We have confidence as to our place and position because we have confidence in Jesus
Christ's invitation to be there and the integrity with which that invitation has been processed.

Our position at the table is delegated. A celebrant at the Lord's Table
is most conscious of this when he or she quotes Jesus at the Thursday
night meal in the Upper Room: "This is my body . . . This is the new . . . ."
The key words, the "punch line" a comic would say is taken away from
the presider. Presiders have nothing to say. Presiding at the Lord's Table
is the most impoverished moment in the presider's vocation: he or she is
speechless when it comes to originality, creativity, eloquence and talent.
Presiders are first receivers of the words because it is a word to them
and for them both as persons in their own right and in their vocational
ministry. Then they are "relayers"—passers on of the words they have
heard. But only the words "received from the Lord."

St. Ambrose of Milan, who baptized St. Augustine, mindful of his delegated place speaks about the words of consecration:

> Consecration by words; by whose words? Those of the Lord Jesus.
> For all the other words which are said previous to this are said by
> the priest: the praises that are offered to God, the prayer that is
> offered for the congregation, for rulers, and for others. But when
> the moment comes to consecrate the venerable sacrament, the priest
> will no longer use his own words, but will use the words of Christ. It is
> therefore the Word of Christ that consecrates this sacrament.[1]

Just so. No celebrant can make the promise made and sealed at the table. Jesus spoke, for example, as Matthew recalls it, of drinking his blood of the Covenant poured out for the forgiveness of sins. Then he promised he would drink again of the vine in a new day in his Father's Kingdom (Matt 26:29). Can any celebrant make such a promise and arouse such hope? As Robert Jenson has noted, every statement humans make is a conditional statement.[2] "We will go on a picnic tomorrow if it does not rain." "I can practice law if I pass the bar exam." And the big contingency, "I will . . . I can . . . if I don't die." At the table the contigent one (the celebrant) is speaking in behalf of the "noncontingent One (Jesus Christ, risen and ascended). If honest, the celebrant will of all persons be most mindful of how contingent he or she is. The words of institution are first words to the celebrant who then has words of promise for those who share the table with him or her. Even at the Table there is the ministry of the word and even when presiding one is a hearer first and speaker second, a guest first and a presider second.

Presence at the Table is shared space. Recall from the previous chapter the reference to the fourteen nationalities at Immanuel Covenant Church in Chicago. Add to this the intentional mission that Jesus instructs his followers to initiate to the persons with disabilities, blindness, deafness and a host of psycho—physical conditions that churches do not usually think of as a priority mission (Luke 14:15–24). Complicate that mission with persons suffering from autism, fragile X syndrome, advanced down syndrome, even among children and youth and what kind of intentionality must a congregation muster to do the ministry of table integration? The Table is the most visible symbol of who is present and who is not. Are those absent, absent because they remain unreached?

1. Quoted from Toal, trans., *Sunday Sermons*, 128.
2. Gritsch and Jenson, *Lutheranism*, 42.

By baptism they have been ascribed the *identity*, Christian, *incorporated* into Christ and *initiated* into this new sociology called People of God, a people made up of peoples! Now the pastoral and congregational task is to *integrate* them into one body. What better way than table fellowship! What more tension—filled way than table fellowship! Table fellowship is the extended sociology of baptism and the intended fruit of the art and science of the development of the priesthood of the congregation.

Both the baptismal maturity and ordinational maturity of the celebrant or lack thereof, come into play in the act of presiding at the Table. The pastoral maturity in terms of spiritual wisdom, knowledge of the biblical narrative and cultural literacy pertinent to the congregation being served go public in the way one serves the socialization process of integrating those initiated into the local Body of Christ. Participation at the Table is a form of the renewal of one's baptism (individual) and the recognition of each other as bonded to each other by water and the Holy Spirit (social). But it continues to work itself out at tables in homes, apartments, shelters, and other diverse locations.

Lest this appear to be so idealistic as to resemble no one's ministry, a look at the post—Easter appearances of Jesus is instructive. Theologically, let my previous points be recalled: Easter is the victory of God who 1) raised Jesus from the dead, 2) vindicated a person given up as a lost cause, vindicated a person accused of false identity claims and was betrayed, sold, and forsaken by his closest friends, and 3) proved himself faithful to Jesus thereby vindicating Jesus' faith in the God of Abraham, Rachel, Hannah, Mary and the host of ancestors. The primary word uttered at Easter is: God can be trusted to keep God's word. The risen Christ is the evidence.

The risen Christ, it turns out, is identical with the crucified Jesus. The crucified Jesus is the risen Christ. But it is an identity in difference. He makes appearances to his disciples in a different body yet with identifiable wounds. When the disciples see the risen Christ they see his wounds. Or do they see their wounds on his body? Mutuallty identifying processes are going on: in seeing the Risen One they are not seeing One who is trying to rub salt in their now freshly evoked bitter memories but the Risen Wounded One still maintains his relations with those who did him in. Just as God vindicated God's promises of fidelity to the Risen One, the Risen One vindicates his word to his fellows: I still want you as my disciples. The Risen One vindicates them as his delegated presiders and preachers. Thus the work of God is continued. God did not let the salvation project collapse but sent the Risen One back to the ones who were most in need of the Risen One's justifying word. Romans 4:25 clearly links the resurrection with the act of justification.

Two derivative applications come to mind. First, the table fellowship of the Risen One, the Wounded with the wounders is a paradigm for congregational eucharists. Participation at the Table is not being present in a wound free zone but a place where, over time, the wounded free the wounders but only after they face the wounds that have been inflicted on fellow communicants or the wounds that persons bring from previous times and places. Such wounded persons may not make for the "smoothest" of relationships. Let it also be said that wounds of varying kinds and sources are subject to varying lengths of healing and should not be subject to the elitist counsel such as "Just move on" or "Aren't you over it yet?" The Table is not our table but the Lord's Table. Let him and his word do its work in the proper way and in the proper time. I cannot imagine a congregational process of integrating the diversity presented in the New Testament and in the examples I have given in this text without wounders and wounded at the same table at the same time. But their One Lord, one faith, one baptism puts them there.

Second, the ordinational maturity to develop the congregational literacy necessary to do this ministry and the spiritual maturity to be humble enough to learn how is a vocational derivative. When pastors preside let it be remembered that between them and their congregants there is bound to be, in some cases, a relationship of wounded and wounder. The traffic moves both ways.

St. John Chrysostom's comments that the Risen One's threefold quizzing of Peter ("Do you love me more than these?" John 21:15–19) is not as existentially oriented as St. Augustine's comments on the same text which I referred to earlier. For St. Augustine the quizzing led to a truthful encounter with the threefold denial and thus a release from guilt. St. John Chrsostom's comments go in a vocational direction.[3] First, the Risen One wanted Peter to know how much he loved the church and the quality of care required for the supervision of the flock that the Risen One had obtained with his own blood. Second, the shepherd needs to know of the spiritual integrity and focus required to protect the flock from the unseen enemies looking for any chance available to access the

3. Chrysostom, *Six Books*, 52–59.

flock, especially by first accessing the shepherd whether by transforming ego to egoism or grievance to grudges. Third, the one focus of the ministry is the edification of the church and it must be carried out without recourse to hostility or favor. The presider also is being quizzed, first and foremost with this question: is the edification of the flock the governing motivation for ministry? And since no ministry is carried out in a wound free zone, is everything being done not to nurture wounds? When the answer is "yes" that is one way of saying, "You know Lord how I love you by how I love your sheep entrusted to me. But you also know how defeated some of your sheep make me feel. Help me to know the difference between loving and liking so that I can serve with integrity even if not always with inspiration."

This poem by Scott Cairns, "All Saints Communion," combines in a way that requires attentiveness, the personal and communal:

> Having accepted from one palsied priest the cool,
> the lucent water, having dipped it duly in the cup,
> I pressed that sweet enormity fast against my tongue
> Where on its sudden dissolution, I received a taste
> of whose I was. I rose again and found my place.

Reflection:
> *Attend to palsied priest yet fully worthy to administer the sacrament.*
> *Sweet enormity—how would you draw that out for yourself?*
> *Taste of whose I was: ascribed identity reaffirmed.*

> As I knelt to pray, I heard a little differently
> the words the priest intoned as he continued offering
> what passed for bread among high Protestants. His words:
> *the body of Christ*, repeated as he set that emblem
> into each pair of out stretched hands. My eyes were shut,[4]

Reflection:
> *I heard a little differently the words . . . Recalling from memory the words of an Episcopal priest lecturing in one of my classes who asked rhetorically, "Why do Episcopalians go to Communion so often?" and answering his own question something like, "It's because by Monday night they've already forgotten who they are!" Or Harry Angstrom, that is, Rabbit in John Updike's novel* Rabbit Is Rich: *"Laugh at ministers all you want: they*

---

4. Cairns, "All Saints Communion," 8.

have the words we need to hear, the ones the dead have spoken."[5] *"I heard a little differently . . . " but what Mr. Cairns heard was the words of the dead one now risen and repeated verbatim by a presider. Same words. But new.*

> so each communicant returning down the aisle became
> something of a shadow illustration of the words. In that
> fraught moment, they became well absorbed into the vast
> array of witnesses, whose cloud invisibly attended
> our sacramental blurring of the edges that keeps us separate.[6]

Reflection:

> *communicant . . . absorbed into the vast array of witnesses*
> *sacramental blurring of the edges that keeps us separate.*

So the becoming one body in Christ through participation in one bread and one cup is a continuing ministry at the Table; a sweet enormity perhaps, too big perhaps except for having received a taste of whose we are.

Just how the communicant-celebrant may come fully to embrace his or her place at the table, I am suggesting a spiritual exercise that "feeds" on the various names for the Table event in a manner that parallels the exercise I suggested with the baptismal images in the New Testament. First, the names for the Table event, some of which may be more connotative than denotative, thus leaving room more for description than definition.

1. A Passover (Matt 26: 17–19; Luke 22:1–5, 14–23; Exod 12)

2. Paschal Feast (1 Cor 5:6–8)

3. The Lord's Supper (1 Cor 11:20)

4. The Last Supper

5. The Holy Communion

6. The Breaking of the Bread (Acts 2:42)

7. The Eucharist (Thanksgiving): Paul and Luke use *eucharisteo* for both bread and cup; Matthew and Mark use *eulogeo* (bless) for bread and cup (1 Cor 11:24, Luke 22:17–19); and *eucharisteo* for the cup (Matt 26:26–27, Mark 14:22–25)

8. The Mass, from the Latin, *mittere*, "to send." At the end of Mass,

5. Updike, *Rabbit is Rich*, 243.
6. Cairns, "All Saints Communion," 8.

the priest said, *Ite missa est*, "The mass is ended," so in effect the ending is a sending, a missionary dispersion.

9. The Marriage Supper of the Lamb (Rev 19:7, 9 and the eschatological theme in 1 Cor 11:26: "For as often as you eat the bread and drink this cup you proclaim the Lord's death until he comes.")

I offer three sketches of meditations as a way of showing what I am suggesting be done as a spiritual exercise.

Let us take the name Last Supper, a name given by tradition for the obvious reason that it was the last meal with the disciples before Jesus died. My meditation draws on Daniel Robb, a teacher of juvenile delinquents at Penikese Island off Cape Cod, a school serving as an alternative to prison. Eight teenagers, virtually daring anyone to teach them anything, and four teachers lived and learned in a familial setting but had to do all the work necessary to live there. Mr. Robb speaks of his initial idealism being eroded over a three-year period, of having best intentions thwarted most of the time although he finds one or two that had some writing potential. But then, almost as a lament, he speaks of not winning at this as he is used to, none of the boys will likely ever visit him, and at the point of leaving he will say "Goodbye" but without closure. He calls this, ". . . exiting in the middle of a meal, in the middle of the day, in the midst of the family discussion . . ."[7]

Is that not a near verbatim account of what the Last Supper must have been like? No closure. The family discussion, especially about betrayal, must have left many loose ends. The whole thing was like the guest had walked out in the middle of a meal. That was the "lastness" of the Last Supper.

But then Easter morning. The beginning of the resumption of the meal although the New Testament tells the story by describing a series of meals, each one a bit more intense than the previous ones (Luke 24:1–41; John 20:28, 21:5, 15ff). Think of Easter as the resumption of the conversation and not the bitter goodbye without closure. Part of the gospel proclamation is that the "Last" Supper has a sequel: the First Supper of Easter (Luke 24).

A second sketchy meditation: The Eucharist. Students of Greek will recognize that the heart of the word for "thanksgiving" is the word for "grace." Gift language dominates. Whatever it is that accompanies re-

7. Robb, "Teacher's Tale," section 14.

ceiving a gift, especially one of a totally unexpected kind for which one feels ill equipped to handle, is set in motion here. But we will err if we stop at the personal, subjective level. Doing so virtually leaves out the biblical mode of thanksgiving.

It is startling to read this sentence from Claus Westermann: "The fact that there is no word for 'to thank' in Hebrew has never been properly evaluated."[8] Westermann shows conclusively how the Western linguistic polarity of "please" and "thank you" are not common ways of showing gratitude, least of all in the Bible. Therein one can only find "praise," which requires paying attention to and then reciting concrete actions back to the person to whom one is trying to express gratitude. Showing gratitude means telling a story, no matter how brief or long, of what has made the relationship significant.

Paul Bradshaw's highly accessible study, *Two Ways of Praying*, devotes a chapter to how the content of Westermann's extensive and detailed exegesis influenced the New Testament prayers and the extant prayers from the patristic period for Baptism, Eucharist, and Ordination, all of which followed the recital or story form. God was praised by reciting his works. When a biblical person prayed, he or she proclaimed the gospel of God by remembering (*anamnesis*—the same word used in the service of the Table) the deeds of God (See Gen 24: 26–27, Exod 18:10–11 and 1 Kgs 8:15–21). Note the beginning key word, "Blessed . . . " is also used by intercessors in the New Testament, Zechariah (Luke 1:68–75) and 1 Peter 1:3. As Bradshaw points out, Christian prayer saw fit to include petitions flowing naturally out of the recitation of God's works.[9] It is likewise well known that the laments were constructed conspicuously noting the *absence* of God's work in the life and times of the intercessor.

A third sketch: Holy Communion. Glen Hinson, patristic scholar of note and of Southern Baptist heritage, has written:

> The Protestant approach did not work out in practice as well as in theory. Perhaps we could say that spiritually, the Protestant faithful were quick to take the bus and leave the driving up to Jesus . . . Behind the problem lay perhaps an inadequate definition of grace, one that emphasized God's acquittal of the sinner at the judgment rather than God's gift of God's self . . . ."[10]

8. Westermann, *Praise and Lament*, 25–30.

9. Bradshaw, *Two Ways of Praying*, ch. 3.

10. Hinson, *Spiritual Preparation*, 58.

I agree, and one reason is that the post-resurrection ministry of Jesus has escaped being a liturgical, theological, or spiritual point of emphasis. "He was raised for our justification," St. Paul proclaims in Romans 4:25. The post-resurrection of ministry of Jesus in the Gospels is one extended pastoral act of restoring betrayers and deserters back to their place in the ministry they had with Jesus. Jesus is justifying their person and service and it begins with the Eucharist in Luke 24 on Easter night. There in person is the gift of God's self, the justifier in person of those who did him in. Justification was not merely a decree made by a judge who then disappeared until the next case was called. The judge made a gift of himself to the accused after their crime. The disciples were not only acquitted, they were accompanied by the judge-justifier.

He proclaimed his justification of the betrayers, not from a bench, but from a table. That is why, in my view, the Eucharist cannot be confined to a memorial meal of the meal in the upper room. It is not in memory of a dead Jesus but an engagement, a communion, with the Risen Jesus Christ. The Table is the proclamation of our justification, the gift of God's very self in the person of his Son, who was not mysteriously raptured from the tomb leaving it empty and the lives of the followers of Jesus even more empty. God raised him and sent him back, and from a table justified the continued discipleship of every one who, by any standard of vocational responsibility, had no reason to be continued in service. Holy Communion with the living Jesus Christ is also with each other in communion with the living Jesus Christ, who is still at work at the Table integrating his often unruly, sometimes rebellious, and sometimes gracious household into a holy human habitat.

Below I have appended two eucharistic prayers of my own composition as an invitation for celebrants to write their own and as meditation on our vocation. Both of them were celebrated at retreats I conducted for seniors at North Park Theological Seminary as part of a way to pray the call process to one's first place of ministry, and hence they are freighted with a specific vocational orientation. Both prayers follow the traditional form of eucharistic prayer.

NORTH PARK THEOLOGICAL SEMINARY CALL TO MINISTRY RETREAT

(The beginning of the process when seniors interview for their first parish call)

Leader:	The Lord be with you
People:	And also with you.
Leader:	Let us give thanks to he Lord, our God.
People:	Which is right and good at all times
Leader:	This season of Lent we render gratitude during the holy season of painful memory; O God, we recall gratefully but regretfully your son's desertion and betrayal by his friends, his public humiliation expediently manipulated by the authorities, and his own struggle with your perceived absence. That he learned obedience through what he suffered is to our comfort and in this identification with us have reason to join all others of our race in heaven and on earth to praise your name saying:

Or in Pentecost:

Leader:	The Lord be with you.
People:	And also with you.
Leader:	Let us give thanks to the Lord, our God.
People:	Which is right and good at all times.
Leader:	This season of Pentecost we give you thanks, O God for the Holy Spirit, the Lord, the giver of life, the bond of unity between you and your Son, Jesus Christ, between us and you, and between ourselves and each other. As this bond becomes more inclusive of others, intensify its integrity. When tested by others, enable its perseverance so that we may join the angels, archangels, and all the company of heaven in praising your name, singing: Holy, holy, holy God of power and majesty Heaven and earth, are full of your glory, O God most high! Blessed is the one who comes in the name of the Lord.

Continuing . . .

Leader:	We give you special thanks for this gathering. We have mixed feelings: about partings; about starting over again; about how to

say what we mean to each other; about ways to find each other if the "between" is lost.

People:	We ask for your mercy and grace, O Lord.
Leader:	God created us in love:
People:	Freely made us after his image and likeness, placed us in communities and families because loneliness was our first enemy and companionship our basic need.
Leader:	God saw this and gave Adam,
People:	Eve;
Leader:	Mary,
People:	Joseph;
Leader:	The Samaritan Woman,
People:	Jesus;
Leader:	Jesus,
People:	Mary, Martha, and Lazarus;
Leader:	Paul,
People:	Barnabas.
Leader:	God takes the solitary and sets them in families.
People:	Praised be God's name!
Leader:	In our loneliness,
People:	Befriend us.
Leader:	In our awkwardness, give us,
People:	Love to reach out and vulnerability to be loved;
Leader:	In dis—ease,
People:	Faith to commit the future to you;
Leader:	In confusion,
People:	Patience to rush to no quick solutions;
Leader:	In silences,
People:	No embarrassment;
Leader:	In anger,
People:	Protection from bitterness;
Leader:	In anxiety,
People:	Your presence;
Leader:	In life,
People:	Honesty to embrace all of our feelings;
Leader:	But especially we recall the love of our Lord Jesus Christ for his own, whom he loved to the end. The ancient words are ever new: On the night he was betrayed he took bread, said the blessing,

broke the bread, and gave it to his friends and said, "Take, eat: This is my Body which is given for you. Do this for the remembrance of me."

After supper, he took the cup of wine, gave thanks, and said, "Drink this, all of you: This is my Blood of the new Covenant, which is shed for you and for many for the forgiveness of sins. Whenever you drink it, do this for the remembrance of me."

People: Mindful of the love that has included us in your grace, enable us to be inclusive of others as we anticipate the day when all things in heaven and on earth will be brought together under one head, even Christ.

Leader: Holy Spirit, unite us, our gifts, our hopes, our ambiguities, and our intentions with Christ who became like us so that we could become like him.

People: That all may see that the transcendent power belongs to you, our Creator, Redeemer, and Friend.

The Acclamation

Leader: Great indeed is the mystery of our faith.
People: Christ has died.
               Christ has risen!
               Christ will come again!

The Lord's Prayer
The breaking of the bread and pouring of the cup
The renewal of our baptisms
The distribution
Sharing
Dismissal and Blessing

Epiphany Season

The Holy Eucharist

Leader: The Lord be with you.
People: And also with you.
Leader: Let us give thanks to the Lord our God.
People: It is indeed right that we do.
Leader: For this, O God, that your Son, Jesus Christ, made in our likeness, freely took the form of a servant for his life's work, found

no one to be unworthy of his life or death, and saw no waste in offering up his life so that others might know unconditional love. Therefore with the angels and archangels and all the company of heaven we praise your name saying . . .

People: Holy, holy, holy
             Lord God of hosts,
             Heaven and earth are full of thy glory,
             Glory be to thee,
             O Lord most high! Amen.

Leader: We continue to thank you, loving God, for those whom you have sent, icons of your presence, prophets of your concern, seers of you future for humankind. For Moses:

People: Sheepwatcher, called by a voice in the bush to see as God sees, to see what God sees, to hear as God hears, to hear what God hears. Give us courage to have open eyes and ears.

Leader: For Hannah:

People: Mother of Samuel the prophet, desolate in childlessness, scorned by those close, yet determined that you hear her out and deliver her. Help us to be active in our waiting and relentness in our praying.

Leader: For Isaiah:

People: Frightened, yet fortified by your holiness; intimidated, yet invited near by your majesty, help us who often despair of your presence to desire it with all of our heart.

Leader: For Jeremiah:

People: Set apart from birth for the service of your work, yet fighting it all the way, protesting, yet praising you. Give us the same honesty with you, and its fruit, hope.

Leader: For Mary:

People: Who knew no reason why she should be the mother of our Lord except that God wanted her. So it is with us. Help us to rest in you, for you alone are our reason for ministry.

Leader: For those within the immediacy of our experience who have made it possible for us to be at this place in life.

People: (Name the names of these people)

Leader: But supremely for Jesus Christ, our chief pastor, who on the night when he was betrayed, took bread, and when he had given thanks, he broke it and said: "This is my body which is for you.

Do this in remembrance of me." In the same way also the cup, after supper, saying: "This cup is the new covenant in my blood. Do this as often as you drink it, in remembrance of me." Great indeed is the mystery of our faith!

People: Christ has died! Christ has risen! Christ is coming again!

Leader: Come upon us, Holy Spirit, and these gifts that by your enabling power we might participate through them in the mystery of the Word become flesh. Christ Jesus our Lord who has been made our wisdom, righteousness and salvation.

Unison: To you, O God, to Jesus Christ and to the Holy Spirit we give praise and thanksgiving for qualifying us to be ministers of the new covenant. Amen

The Lord's Prayer
The breaking of the bread and pouring of the cup
The renewal of our baptisms
The distribution
Sharing
Dismissal and Blessing

7

What Language Shall
I Borrow?

Learning to Pray by Borrowing from Scripture

IN THE CHRISTIAN COMMUNITY, the Bible is the central book. It is read liturgically in the congregation, devotionally by persons and families, pedagogically in church school classes, and technically in theological seminaries.

Bible reading gets mixed reviews. For some it is a source of great comfort. For others, the Bible generates conflict, sometimes for textual content, sometimes for language use, and sometimes because its distant culture renders it alien. Bible reading is labor intensive, emotionally taxing, and intellectually challenging. Given such matters it is easy to concede the Bible to the experts whose expertise supposedly mitigates such demands. For Christians, it is the basic narrative of living with God.

The purpose of this chapter is to be suggestive of some ways that pastors and spiritual guides may use texts to foster healthy ways to live with God, for themselves as well as others. When persons relate stories of intensifying ambiguities in the life of faith and inhibiting ambivalences in seeking to be faithful, they will find themselves in good biblical company! The characters who populate the biblical narratives found themselves in conflict with the same God who was their source of comfort (Job 13:15; Ps 22:1–3). When persons plead uniqueness, there is a companion in a text who can speak the same language. More importantly, this companion can encourage persons to find their voice in praying their own words.

I begin with stories. They are not as remote as one might think. In spiritual direction these stories are not read for their educational value, significant as that is. These stories are read for their power to mirror the reader, to face the face in the mirror. Biblical stories are "borrowed" for their revelatory power. So are the stories of other Christians, technically designated as hagiography, or the lives of the saints. They too, have mirroring power.

|

Biblical stories may be used to frame a person's story. Bible stories are rich in parallels to human situations. Those serving as spiritual companions will find their effectiveness made more versatile by being able to use these stories as frames for those companioned in their efforts to engage God. Persons being companioned sometimes feel that their situations are "unique" and therefore are exceptions to the rule. Others may feel shame that they have the sentiments they do against God, self, and others, rendering them unfit to pray for or about anything. A spiritual loneliness of the worst kind may gradually isolate such persons depriving them of any sense of connection with the community of faith.

I have learned the use of framing in a variety of ways. First, Dr. Dianne Komp, a pediatric oncologist associated with Yale Medical School, describes her spiritual care of parents and families negotiating their way through the terminal illnesses of one of their children. She notes that "over the years . . . the three passages they study and restudy are Jesus in the Garden of Gethsemane, the story of Job, and the story of Abraham on Mount Moriah." Komp explains that parents tend to see such illnesses through the lens of parental failure. When such memories remain unforgiven they "return unbidden to challenge our view of life and our views of God." She concludes, "God, the Parent who so loved the world, became a co-sufferer with all parents who share Abraham's supreme test of faith (Gen 22), through the gift and death of his beloved Son."[1] I find it a reversal of sorts. The parent did not choose texts of immediate comfort or of overt promises. The three stories helped them

---

1. Komp, "Hearts Untroubled," xlv.

grieve and placed them in a "community" of grieving persons. The Bible granted permission to grieve without the slightest hint of guilt. Hope had to await its time.

Second, let us suppose a person who has begun to minister in a hospice, in shelters for the abused such as I previously related, or in clinics for the poor. The person in question seeks guidance because, as the ministry proceeds, the person feels less and less adequate to the task, increasingly feels muted by the questions of the persons, the enormity of the suffering, and finally wonders if he or she had totally misread their perceived call to such a ministry. An approach one could take to such a person would be to ask what biblical story might illumine the situation. After rehearsing a number of stories, the life of Abraham might be found to be a fit. Abraham left a people, place, and language (Ur of the Chaldeans and then Haran) to go to a place he and his kin had never seen, to a new language and set of customs (Canaan; Gen 12). Using the imagination, look at some parallels: 1) leaving one's comfort zone and its familiar peoples and scheduled life; 2) entering a new land, learning the "new language" by presence, by listening more than speaking; 3) apprehending the questions, not as detached philosophy, but as persons seeking to be a listener first and then a response that is not an explanation; 4) by learning how to be at home, of not being defensive or resistant when one's inadequacy seems very real; 5) by recognizing that part of being made adequate is a gift from the persons visited: they give the listener language, the words, the fears, and the hopes, and with that comes the permission to the hearer to use that same language in dialogical conversation; and 6) like Abraham and his kin, one learns that all of this is "By faith . . . " (Heb 11:8–12). Much of ministry is an "Abrahamic" journey where one claims no expertise and knows firsthand the drawing power of the obedience of faith. Ordinational maturation is a vocational name for this process.

Third, I gave myself some spiritual direction by the *lectio* method in August 1982 during the painful time of having to commit my parents to a nursing home. By that time they were unable to participate in the decision. Being an only child makes decision-making only more isolated. My method of journaling is to note the calendar date and the season of the liturgical calendar. My view is that Christians live in two time zones: this age and the age to come. In this age we go from birth to death but in the age to come, present already if only by promise, we go from death to life. Hence I always note the two time zones: Pentecost/Trinity and August 1982.

> This has been a vexing summer. Mother and Dad have suffered pronounced decline in mind and body. I'm in the process of having to move them to Brandel Care Center. Body functions are no longer under control. Dad is oblivious at times as to who is there and what is going on. Mom forgets. She has no sense of time and can hardly make the bed; she does not do the laundry.
>
> It is a strange spot to be in: to take over the destiny of the two people whom you love very much. In some ways it seems to be a contradiction of love, that is, love doesn't appear to want to take over the destiny of others. John Macquarrie defines love as "letting be."[2] This whole thing is a profound encounter with how love acts in apparently contradictory ways in order to remain love. If they were just "let be" it could be destructive to them, debilitating to their general health and demeaning to their person—the senile easily become spectacles—how tragic. So love takes over and acts.
>
> That brings about reversal. A son who is subject to parents and is to be submissive to their authority now becomes the one who exercises authority, control and destiny. Such power is dangerous because those over whom power is exercised are vulnerable and defenseless. They can get by on so little. Get by. That's a temptation—to cut corners on expenses for comforts and amenities. To cut corners on time—they don't really know. They are truly subject to me. Necessarily they are and must be subject but not subjugated.
>
> However weak, however fragile, however impotent, however unimpressive no matter they are subjects and subject, but are not to be subjugated. Even should they lose their mind totally, subjects but not subjugated. A fine line, but necessary for their protection and mine.
>
> All of this brings to mind Jesus' conversation with St. Peter during Easter, (St. John 21:18): "Truly, Truly, I say to you, when you were young you girded yourself and walked where you would; but when you are old you will stretch your hands and another will gird you and carry you where you do not want to go." So true.

The value in this act of writing was that I wrote myself to clarity. When I came to see the distinction between "subject to" but not

---

2. Macquarrie, *Principles*, 144.

"subjugated" I had a measure of freedom to act. Given their physical and mental condition their agency in the matter was precluded. But their personhood was not. They were subject to me for the sake of their personhood, their dignity, their care, but not subjugated as if they were now only ciphers. They were still my parents. It was my vocation to honor them.

Finally, two stories have served me as frames for specific situations. First Samuel 1 relates the story of the infertility of Hannah, of her vulnerable standing in her family system and her freedom to cry out desperately to the God who, the story says, had "closed her womb." Reading this with those who endure similar situations encourages them to speak to God with the same intensity and integrity as Hannah did. Psalm 113, which bears some relation to Hannah's praise in 1 Samuel 2:1–10, is a lyrical exaltation of God who even dwells with the most excluded of persons on the city dumps. Echoes of this psalmic material are found in the Virgin Mary's hymn in Luke 1:46–55.

The story of the woman and her son driven out of Abraham's and Sarah's household found in Genesis 21:15–21 is a dwelling place for mothers and children who have been forced out of their homes. Hagar and Ishmael could suitably bear the names of many modern persons without any sense of falsification. In my own ministry this story has been chosen to convey such circumstances. Despite provisions sufficient to sustain life, the bitterness of the experience is not easily assuaged. I could hear a directee's appeal for Hagar and Ishmael to become part of a support system, able to sustain in part what even bread and water cannot. There is no substitute for a sustaining companionship with persons who know the issue and language from the inside. There is nothing worse than to have people say, "I understand" who have never stood under the burden that is being carried. Hagar and Ishmael know the situation from the adult perspective and the perspective of youth. Imagine the constructive dialogue that could be opened up between a directee, Hagar and Ishmael. An exercise could be devised to structure such a dialogue.

II

Versatility in forms and language of prayer is a basic need of a person. If all a person has heard is to address God in male and hierarchical words, then the scripture can become a repertoire of language fit for borrowing. If the person's experience with persons in authority, especially in religious settings, has been hurtful, then one may access the nurturing images. If prayer is a new experience for the person, then it can be instructive and inspiring to eavesdrop on another prayer.

When reading the Bible keep a notebook at hand. Write down each new word or image that is descriptive of God. Two things need to be said about such word pictures. They are not concepts of God to be memorized like long catechetical answers—"God is the being greater than which none can be conceived" (Anselm). Descriptive words are images drawn from experiences. Concepts can be taught. Images are evoked. Concepts rely on long sentences because they strive for as complete a definition as possible. Images are a word or two NOT turned into a definition. Images are like a collage: all the pieces are there but they are not constitutive of an exact reproduction.

When it comes to addressing God in prayer, images function in two ways. On the one hand, they project one's view of God in terms derivable from one's experience. Such images are often drawn from experiences of power, sense of worth, relation to parents, authority figures, and situations in life where significant persons either did or did not care appropriately. On the other hand, these images project the way one might perceive that God views us and the ways God deals with us. Mature prayer grows ever aware of these projections, their sources and, like the biblical ancestors, turns these projections into prayer, into matters of negotiation with God. Images used for God, drawn from experience, relate to three powerful forces: belonging, goodness, and control. Since these three are raised to their ultimate value in God, the imaging of God is no small matter.[3]

The more diverse the portfolio of images, the richer the relationship and the more versatile the possibilities of prayer. Any relationship, be it with God or humans, goes through its times of intimacy and distance, ecstasy and humiliation, testing and triumph, satisfaction or lack

3. The reflections in these paragraphs have their source in a paper given by Richard Lawrence, "God's Image and Self Image," at the Society for the Scientific Study of Religion, Pittsburgh, October 20, 1991.

thereof. A notebook filled with such a range of images will reveal to the recorder that the people who inhabit biblical narratives have gone through the same range of human experience. All of life is prayable. The more diverse the language of prayer the more one can access the various sectors of one's life.

Some examples are in order. Isaiah 49:15 depicts God as a nursing mother who cannot forget the child of her womb. But a nursing mother also has a task that is laden with ambiguity for mother and child: weaning. Psalm 131:2 hints at the result of the weaning process completed: the weaned child can even lie at mother's breast with no need to nurse. But to get to that point the mother had to begin the process of weaning. The child no doubt fought it and the mother puzzled at why such stressful, often painful efforts needed to be made. In the process and afterward, the child needed to know that such a process of separation would not lead to abandonment. To use words of John Bowlby, the pioneer of attachment theory, the person is moving and being moved to embrace both attachment and detachment in new ways, hopefully defined more and more by trust.[4]

The ambivalence of the divine-human relationship is noted in Deuteronomy 32:11 via the mother eagle who stirs her nest, edging the eaglets toward the open air and their first experience of flight or fall. Yet there she is with that extensive wingspan—support, security, and strength. Nevertheless, the supportive mother is the same one who stirs the nest. In terms of this section, could one not pray to God, ambivalent though one's feelings might be and as ambiguous as God's ways might seem, as questions: Are you weaning or abandoning, stirring or shoving?

For more celebrative times, there are those magnificent pictures of God as rock (Deut 32:4, 18; Ps 144:2), as steadfast in love (Pss 129:7, 117; 118:1–3), as redeemer (Pss 19:14; 25:22; Isa 50:2), as strength (Pss 27:1; 73:26), as comforter (maternal, Isa 66:13), as advocate (John 14:16; 15:26), to name a few. When deliverance came, God was often named according to the provision. In Genesis 22, God is named as the one who provides and in Exodus 18:10 God is the one who makes a way out of bondage.

---

4. Cited from Sylva, *Psalms*, 35. Bowlby's words are distributed throughout, beginning on p. 35.

Some texts beg to be borrowed and prayed as they are! Two examples of such patterns of prayer are Psalm 70:1 and "the Jesus Prayer." How might one do so is the subject of the next section.

III

Psalm 70:1 reads: "Be pleased, O God, to deliver me. O Lord, make haste to help me" (NRSV). When John Cassian (360–475) inquired after the monastic practice of praying without ceasing, this psalm verse was the answer. It could be prayed making baskets or preparing a meal. He speaks of it as a formula for piety passed down from the fathers. Prayed unceasingly, this prayer is an indomitable wall for those struggling against demons; the sturdiest of shields, an impenetrable breastplate; when things go well it is a warning not to be proud. He specifies six capacities to be associated with this prayer.

> "It carries with it all the feelings of which human nature is capable."
>
> "It can be adapted to every condition and can be usefully deployed against every temptation."
>
> "It carries with it a cry for help to God in the face of every danger."
>
> "It expresses the humility of a pious confession."
>
> "It conveys watchfulness born of unending worry and fear."
>
> "It conveys a sense of our frailty, the assurance of being heard, the confidence in help that is always and everywhere present."[5]

It almost seems that Cassian puts more weight on this text than it can bear, like promising more than can be delivered. The key lies in its repetition: there is no circumstance in life in which this prayer does not ring true. But for Cassian, even if one came into great inheritance, received a job of a lifetime, or had a life of exceeding one's dreams, one especially needed to pray Psalm 70:1. No situation in life is exempt from the Lord's mercy, be it from embitteredness, from false security, or pride rooted in an assumed imperviousness to the dark side of life.

Some may protest that this repeated use of the same words is a violation of Jesus' warning against vain repetition of religious formulae used by the "religious professionals" of his time. My view is that a wise

---

5. Cassian, *Conferences*, 10.10.

spiritual director can point out that, as Cassian advocates their use, the words stay the same but the prayer changes according to the person's circumstances. Pleas for God's mercy in prosperity can be distinguished from pleas for mercy in dire circumstances. Same words, different prayer.

A second form of praying the same words yet praying a different prayer comes with the use of the Jesus Prayer, more or less in this form: "Lord Jesus Christ, Son of God, have mercy on me." This prayer has three specific textual sources, each of them phrasing the prayer slightly differently: a blind beggar outside the city walls of Jericho cried out, "Jesus, Son of David, have mercy on me!" (Mark 10:47). A Canaanite woman, an outsider with a distressing physical condition, cried out, "Have mercy on me, O Lord, Son of David" (Matt 15:22). Ten lepers, living in a border community of mixed ethnic and religious composition, cried out, "Jesus, Master, have mercy on us" (Luke 17:13). Per-Olof Söjgren says that what distinguishes this prayer is that it is not for any thing or gift but for mercy and tenderheartedness, constitutive of a relationship with God that can be healthy and hopeful.[6]

This prayer acquires added depth when the narratives embodying the prayers are read and meditated. Mercy means something different to each of them. Each of the petitioners suffered social exclusion for different reasons, but especially the lepers and the Canaanite women. That Jesus should associate with them, even heal them also meant that their social exclusion was over. Mercy had something to do with the risk Jesus took to be with them, to use touch, to show what the late Bishop J. A. T. Robinson called "the human face of God." As Christian people pray this prayer, in whatever circumstances, Jesus is a bridge: between God and oneself and between oneself and God.[7]

The dexterity of the Jesus Prayer shows itself when it is prayed by persons under stress as a breath prayer. By correlating inhaling and exhaling with the words, one is surprised by how measurably one's breathing slows, the heart rate follows and the person begins to be able to release the stress. Follow this practice, seated in a relaxed position:

Breathe in	Breathe out
Lord Jesus,	Son of God
Have Mercy,	on Me

6. Sjögren, *Jesus Prayer*, 18.

7. Ibid., 83.

Theologically, there is significant biblical and therefore fruitful spiritual practice that emerges from this biblical narrative coherence.

1. Humans live by "borrowed" breath. God breathed breath into the first humans. Breath is a gift.

2. Breath is a sign of human mortality. Breath is eventually "lost."

3. Post-Easter, Jesus breathed on the disciples and said, "Receive the Holy Spirit."
   A gift that is the sign of a new creation.

4. To use prayer as a way to coordinate the biospiritual, therefore, is a perfectly good thing to do, linking creation with redemption in the task of healing the person.

The point is, God's very own self is extended to any who cry out for mercy, using body and spirit, even as the words stay the same and the prayer changes. Diverse texts can be formed into a collage and in that maneuver find their unity in the lived–experience of the one who prays.

IV

A final use of scriptural texts in spiritual direction derives from the work of the French priest and social worker the Reverend Michel Quoist. This method has three parts: an experience or encounter in the course of one's life, ministry, or work; several bible texts that connect with this experience (a concordance might be helpful here so that one can locate the occurrences of various names or words in their various biblical contexts); and a written meditation, reflection, or prayer that joins the experience and the biblical passages.

An example might be Quoist's encounter with the Paris phonebook. Entering a phone booth and searching for a number, he found himself dealing with all the names! Each was a story. Each had hopes and regrets. But nearly all of them were anonymous to him. But not to God! God knows my name. And these names! God's knowing restores some sense of the personal and relational. God does not look for numbers. They have no story. God looks for names and enters a story!

Quoist then lists five or so texts that say something about names. For this second part of the exercise he gives no commentary. Given some time and use of a concordance one can begin to note the range of texts that deal with names and then discern those that most fit with the experience.

Finally, Quoist integrates these texts with the experience. His method is to write a prayer meditation that integrates the texts with the experience.[8] The form of the integrative meditation (journal entry, poem, photo essay, musical lyrics) is the person's choice. The faithful practice of this discipline bears fruit in a prayed life.

I "borrowed" the title from Paul Gerhard (1607–1676).[9] All of us, pastors and parishioners, guides and guided, are welcome to borrow stories and words of scripture to equip us in our effort to engage God. We may also discover that God works at borrowing our speech in order to engage us.

RESOURCES

1. Jeanette Bakke, *Holy Invitations: Exploring Spiritual Direction* (Baker, 2000)
2. David Benner, *Sacred Companions: The Gift of Spiritual Friendship and Direction*, forward by Larry Crabb (InterVarsity, 2002)
3. Margaret Guenther, *Holy Listening: The Art of Spiritual Direction*, forward by Alan Jones (Cowley 1992)
4. Thelma Hall, *Too Deep for Words: With 500 Scripture Texts for Prayer* (Paulist, 1998)
5. Thomas Keating, *The Better Part: Stages of Contemplative Living*, especially chapters 1, 2, and 4 (Continuum, 2000)
6. Richard Peace, *Contemplative Bible Reading: Experiencing God through Scripture* (Navpress, 1998)
7. Richard Peace, *Meditative Prayer: Entering God's Presence.* (Navpress, 1998)
8. Eugene Peterson, *Working the Angles: The Shape of Pastoral Integrity*, especially chapters 1–6 (Eerdmans, 1987)

8. Quoist, *Prayers.*

9. From stanza 3 of "O Sacred Head, Now Wounded," translated by James Alexander, as found in the *Covenant Hymnal*, 238.

Coda

Made Healthy in Ministry by Ministry

O NE OF THE FRUITS of being made healthy in ministry by ministry is a certain detachment but not indifference. To be indifferent would be to be satisfied with clerical professionalism carried out to a tee, a contract fulfilled in every detail, to view ministry primarily in job/career terms with an eye to the next level. The indifference comes in, in that one's sight is set just beyond where one is serving. What one sees in the end is oneself being served by the ones one is supposedly called to serve. An indifferent pastor can be very "personable" but where is the person? What kind of sacramental presence (or absence) is such a pastor?

As for detachment, which I distinguish from indifference, may I try a personal reflection? I no longer pray for God to bless my ministry. When I came to appropriate in some more mature fashion the promise that God will not let his Word return to him empty, I relaxed and felt delivered from a kind of imprisoning subjectivity. I was freed to let God do God's work when God knew the time was right. Thus I was freed to do my work for which I was ordained: preach the Word, administer the Sacraments and let them, under the power of the Holy Spirit, work. As I tried to show in the previous chapters, these lead to significant avenues of pastoral care and pastoral leadership as a way of "bearing rule in the church." Recall the pastor as "discernmentarian"?

So my prayers now are of gratitude for God's promise and for the freedom to minister with a sense of detachment. I cannot make the Word work. But I can watch for signs and hints that the seed is sprouting and when perhaps the person is ready for whatever the next stage of intentional ministry requires. And I can cultivate the soil in which other people are "planted" whether it means crisis intervention, legal advocacy, companioning, even critical conversation in order that the seed of the Word can take root. But then I thank God for God's promise because that is my reason to stay in ministry. And that is my reason, as stated in Chapter 1, for placing so much stock in Galatians 5:6, namely that faith acts in love and not love acting in faith. Love is easily short—circuited. Faith waits for God to act and thus faith sustains love. So it is that "detachment" in faith acting in love frees one to serve the present time. It turns out that this "detachment" is, paradoxically, rooted in a deep form of attachment to one's ministry and so health has a chance to be maintained by ministry in ministry.

Yet even this God whose promises I have so much treasured is not without mystery. Just because promises have been made regarding Word and Sacrament does not mean that everything has been explained, every suffering justified, every question made answerable and every human situation hospitable.

A vocational hazard is precisely the God we serve. Some of God's ways are inscrutable. In such times we live by promise, fully attached to ministry and promise, fully detached by promise but always by faith acting in love. Take Isaiah as a case in point.

Isaiah is called in a dramatic encounter described in Isaiah 6:1–6. After this intimidating yet inviting encounter with the Holy One, he is sent to preach *but* with some words no preacher would want to hear. Tell them to "Keep listening, but do not comprehend; keep looking, but do not understand. Make the mind of this people dull and stop their ears, and shut their eyes so that they may not look with their eyes, and listen with their ears and comprehend with their minds, and turn and be healed" (9–10). Talk about a vocational crisis! Amos was told that a famine would be sent, not of food but of hearing the word of the Lord (8:11). Why preach?

The matter is intensified by Jesus whose use of Isaiah 6 appears in both Matthew 13 and Mark 8. Jesus is interpreting the difficulty of understanding parables and in Matthew the difficulty is attributed to fulfillment of prophecy. Mark's use makes it a bit more difficult for the preacher in that the act of telling seems to be part of the obscuring process. Jesus does not allude to the end of Isaiah 6 which speaks of a seed alive in a stump left over from a major era of destruction.[1] Jesus does refer to a variety of soils and a mixed harvest.

My point is that in a media savvy culture that is market driven and forever autopsied by focus groups in search of the communication format that will get results, these biblical texts need to be heard. The Word of God is not subject to any human control and preachers — some readers of this work among them — just might be called with Isaiah's commission. There may indeed be sent a famine of hearing the Word of God. But I know of no place in scripture where a famine of preaching was sent! Why? Because there must be a seed left in the stump, just as after the flood there had to be the seedlings of the new creation, "the little seed vessel that was the ark" as St. Peter Chrysologus called it.[2]

So brothers and sisters in the ministry, even when living with God becomes the mystery of the ministry, when God's ways defy all norms, we can remain detached from ministry while remaining attached to ministry because even when God assigns us to a time of famine of hearing God's word, God assigns us to planting time with the promise: My word will not return void but will accomplish that for which I sent it. The seed is in the stump. Watch for it. Nourish it with water. Sustain it with bread and wine. Pulpit, font or pool and table: locations of ministry made hopeful by promise. To your health!

1. Wright, *Jesus*, 236–37.

2. Chrysologus, *Selected Sermons*, 281.

Addendum I

A Partial Sketch of Lay Ministry

THE PURPOSE OF THIS book is concerned with the vocational health of those in the course of their ministry. Since pastoral ministry is a correlate of the ministry of the people of God and not an end in itself, I want to show how I would have developed a more comprehensive pastoral theology. I am offering a modest and abbreviated prospectus on one aspect of the development of ministry of the laity in one congregation I served, from 1970 to 1975, namely the Evangelical Covenant Church of Princeton, Illinois. In terms of the language of the book, this is a component of the baptismal maturation of the people of God as it is effected in their diverse ministries and implementation of gifts in a parish setting.

I. BASIS BIBLICAL AND THEOLOGICAL ASSUMPTIONS

A. The pastor equips the saints for the work of ministry (Eph 4).

B. Charisms have been distributed by the Holy Spirit to be discerned and trained for service (1 Cor 12:14).

C. By baptism the people of God have entered the priestly service with the people of God (narrative coherence biblically with Exodus 19 and 1 Peter 2 and theologically with Luther and Spener, our particular ancestors in the faith).

    D. Pastoral theology is the art and science of the development of the priesthood of the congregation.

II. IMPLEMENTATION

A. A survey of the entire community by a committee of ten (teenager to senior citizen) to ascertain at what points congregants (individuals or groups) could serve in some capacity. A sheet of paper, single-spaced on both sides, was returned noting points at which immediate service could begin. There was no lack of mission field!

B. Five Steps

    1. Determine needs (survey)

    2. Determine resources available in the congregation

    3. Link persons with places to be served

    4. Train according to placement

    5. Support system for the people in ministry

C. Because this required considerable pastoral availability and time (I was serving alone but with the assistance of a valued volunteer lay administrative associate), the diaconate assumed greater ministerial responsibility.

    1. Deacons called twice a week in the hospital to supplement pastoral calling. Training by role-playing a variety of calling situations was held annually.

    2. Holy Communion was distributed four times a year to the people unable to attend worship. I celebrated the Eucharist in the church with the eight who would be serving, and wrote a service of distribution and a letter of greeting to each home visited.

    3. A grief ministry of visitation was formed for weekly visits in homes where death had happened.

    4. Visitation to the homes of newcomers to Princeton.

    5. Some training in how to minister to disaffected church members.

D. This is my way, in part, of the art and science of the development of the priesthood of the congregation flowing from and to the Word and Sacraments.

Addendum II

Toward Self-Care

I AM RECOMMENDING THREE BOOKS of differing purposes. The book I have written may come across as too individualistic. It need not. It may be read in a group. Some of the exercises suggested may be so done.

Rochelle Melander and Harold Eppley, *The Spiritual Leader's Guide to Self-Care*. Forward by Roy W. Oswald. Bethesda, MD: Alban Institute, 2002.

Contains an exercise per week for a year. Each exercise has a design for connecting with oneself, a partner, and God. No area of personal or vocational life is omitted.

Gary L. Harbaugh. *Pastor as Person: Maintaining Personal Integrity in the Choices and Challenges of Ministry*. Minneapolis: Augsburg, 1984.

Each chapter has a case study that concerns some form of personal and pastoral integrity. Professor Harbaugh is adapt at the integration of theology and psychology.

Dean R. Hoge and Jacqualine E. Wenger. *Pastors in Transition: Why Clergy Leave Local Church Ministry*. Grand Rapids: Eerdmans, 2005.

Includes not only the seven main motivations for leaving ministry, but also a section on perspectives from judicatory leaders. The interviews are extensive and the interpretive material useful.

Addendum III

Some Suggested Spiritual Exercises, to Be Done Preferably in Conversation with Others

I. The Reverend Dr. David Kersten, the Executive Minister of the Board of the Ordered Ministry of the Evangelical Covenant Church, reported to me a conversation which originated from his work with the Midwest Ministry Development Center. With his consent, I am reporting two questions in summary form which the center says are necessary for any clergyperson to face and answer with integrity:

A. At what point can one recognize one's incompetence?

B. At what places is one fraudulent?

What resources from being a *hearer* of the Word and *recipient* of the Sacraments enable you to face these questions so that your spiritual health can sustain the integrity of your ministry?

II. What narratives can be shared that show the development of "ordinational maturity" (chapter 3)?

III. With regard to the intellectual aspects of ministry, that which asks us to love God with the mind requires integrity of mind. Try this for conversation. In the course of my reading I came across the work in astronomy by MIT scientist Alan Guth, who inquires that if the universe comes from nothing, what meaning is there? He further avers that this undermines the belief that we are here for a cosmic purpose. At the same time it does not mean that our lives are meaningless. What do you think about separating purpose from meaning (chapter 2)?

IV. Take the issue of criticism, which can range from occasional to being nearly epidemic. How to handle it? Milton B. Copenhaver, in "Slings and Arrows" (*Christianity Century*, June 16, 2009), writes of his own experience with both criticism and praise, which he labels as "twin imposters," because both can deceive and mislead. Both are rooted in caring for God's people, including what they think yet not caring too much, otherwise how could one survive?

He advocates growth in confidence in one's gifts and deeper clarity that ministry is not about oneself, as a cello cannot accept praise for a sonata. Furthermore, when criticism is taken too seriously, one can feel nibbled to death. When praise is taken too seriously, one may end up seeking it. "Praise may be a fitting reward, but it is a misleading motivation."

In addition to discussing Copenhaver's point, work at a question posed to me: What to do, how to respond when criticism is epidemic? What is self-care in that setting?

V. Talk about the difference between "faith active in love" versus "love active in faith" as an approach to pastoral service and the long-term effects in the spiritual life (chapter 1).

VI. How much freedom for ministry do we know because of the promise of God concerning God's word (see the Coda)?

VII. Does this freedom include the freedom to live with God with the same integrity that biblical persons did (chapter 1)?